ONE YEAR OF REALITY AND HOW IT NEARLY KILLED ME

My Life Behind the Scenes

Thanks for helping me!

Deborah

Deborah M Wolff

Copyright © 2015 Deborah M Wolff
All rights reserved.

ISBN: 1511867159
ISBN 13: 9781511867153

ACKNOWLEDGMENTS

I have to start by thanking my family, particularly my mother, who was a great support through everything and who silently sacrificed for me. Not a day goes by that I do not remember her generosity to me and to those around her. I can only hope to be like her someday. She was a light to many people.

I also have to thank my closest friends who helped me when I had nowhere else to go: Rhonda, Kelly, and Stacy. There is not enough time in this life to ever repay you for your kindness and friendship. You are my sisters, and I love you dearly. And to Laura, thanks for the extra ear and dose of sanity, for being my "other brain." You are the best. And a special thank you to Angela Polidoro for editing the book.

I am truly blessed. I got into the entertainment industry for two reasons. One, I wanted to be an actress, and two; I wanted to wear jeans and T-shirts to work. Well, one out of two isn't bad. In my work and play, I have encountered fabulous people and colleagues I am grateful to know. The people on the production side of media are workhorses who daily put in the hours and labor to make content for all to enjoy.

Finally, I'd like to thank the Academy…☺

PROLOGUE

5:30 a.m. Downtown Los Angeles. Half-awake. It was a B Stunt day on *Fear Factor*, meaning that it was a food challenge, and all the contestants would have to eat something gross. I walked to the dance hall to make sure the location was "safe." And after making sure that the steadicam guy could manage the stairs with his rig, I started to head over to the catering truck for breakfast, deep in thought about how the day would unfold. As I walked the few blocks to the catering truck, I was looking through my show binder, flipping through paperwork, call sheets, and schedules for the day. I wasn't paying too much attention to anything other than what was in my binder.

Then my ankle twisted and I started to fall in slow motion.

I fought the fall, trying to stay upright. I'm 6'2", and as I've always joked, it's a long way to the ground. That joke is a lot less funny when you actually do find yourself falling. I lost the fight to stay on my feet that morning, and I found myself on the ground in a lot of pain.

I saw people across the street and yelled for help. Everything was blurry as my glasses had come off, but I could see figures walking. No one came to my aid. I yelled a few more times, hearing my voice echo on the almost deserted street. I felt the burn of pain running through my body, and from the corner of my eye, I could see that my right arm was twisted in the wrong direction. I finally yelled, "Somebody in catering, HELP!" After another moment, some of the staff finally came to my aid. I heard someone say, "I thought you were a homeless guy." And then I started hearing people talking into walkies asking for help. All the noise and even the pain started to fade from my mind after a moment, lost in a storm of thoughts about everything—my life, how I would pay for the ambulance, my career... Did I make the right decisions? Was my career over? Did I even have a career? Was I wearing underwear? When would they give me some pain killers? Where was the medic from the show??? My life flashed before my eyes...

One Year of Reality and How It Nearly Killed Me

It's pretty amazing the way the body shuts itself down so you can manage whatever you're going through. I only wish it would've shut my brain off too. This was the last straw in an otherwise amazing year of working on reality TV shows. I was able to work on three different shows from three different networks, and I went through a trial by fire on each one. I remember a producer's assistant telling me, "If they only had the cameras on you, what a reality show it would be."

How had I ended up here, on the ground? What choices had I made that led to this?

CHAPTER 1
LONG BEFORE I HIT PAVEMENT

It all started when I was a kid; I had a dream of going to Africa. I wrote a lengthy essay about the Congo in the sixth grade. I went to the library with my mom and picked out every book about Africa, combing through the World Book Encyclopedias at home and any other books I could find for more information. I was just fascinated by Africa—the beauty, the people and culture. I'm sure my teacher wasn't looking for a ten page essay, but my paper channeled my passionate wish to travel the world. I had often thought about becoming a missionary or working for the Peace Corps.

Fast forward twenty-five years, a few years before I ended face up on the pavement, waiting for an ambulance.

I finally got closer to my dream of going to Africa when I was hired to work for a wildlife show that was my entre into reality television called *Wild Things*. The show did not have a host or narrator like many animal shows—rather, the cameras followed around individuals who worked with wildlife, telling their stories and the stories of the animals they studied. By the end of the show, viewers would learn a little bit about the person as well as the animal. It was both educational and entertaining. I started behind the scenes as a coordinator. It was my first freelance gig in a number of years, so I was nervous about entering the production workforce after leaving a "safe" studio job for one that had no stability. But my "safe" job was boring and predictable, and it was probably coming to an end anyway, since the studio was changing ownership. I took a risk to leave and it paid off big time.

My interview had been with the executive producer, Bert, and the executive in charge, Mark. Bert was a handsome older man, very charismatic and energetic. The kind of person who was so convincing that you'd believe cows flew if he told you it was true. He wanted to make sure I had the experience needed to do an international show. I felt like I was in a poker game. We were sizing each other up and I didn't want there to be any "tells" that I couldn't handle the job because of my lack of experience. I rattled off some countries that I may or may not have experience with, just to spruce up my image. It was true that I had some experience working with Canada and had done research for filming in other countries, but I probably didn't have the kind of experience I should've had to get the job. Occasionally I read about filming in other countries and even had to get a passport updated for an actor on a movie, but that was about it. So I was slightly out of my element. But I squeaked by enough to get hired. Bert and I got along very well in the beginning, and I felt that camaraderie most of the time I was there, but we did have our moments.

There was the executive in charge, Mark, who I liked to call the "Big Cheese." He was young, confident, handsome, and funny—a great guy to work with and learn from. Over the three years we worked together, he taught me a lot about budgets, dealing with people, and even picking stocks. He was very proud of his financial prowess and his meteoric rise to his position. I respected him greatly and wished very much to be like him. I consider him my mentor to this day.

The one person that I started a long lasting friendship with was Laura, the accountant on the show. We got along right away, primarily because she liked my jokes and thought I was funny. To this day we are good friends. She was someone I could talk to about anything and ask for advice on how to deal with office politics or with people in general. She came up with a phrase that I still use to this day. "It's not your fault; it's just your turn."

The best and hardest aspect of *Wild Things* was the fact that it was an international production. We needed people from all over the world to assist in the production, and we were constantly sending staff and crew overseas. As the rest of the team was assembled, I realized that I probably had the least international experience of anyone.

Some of the staff had great international resumes. I remember a field producer who knew everything about Russia; she was incredible. And we also had people on the staff from other countries. There was a small group of us that had a small amount of international experience—well, a *tiny* bit in my case. I came from a studio background, an office environment where I had not been directly involved in production.

One of the biggest things I had to learn was to use an atlas, because we were going to travel all over the world. My chief job responsibilities were to travel the crews and producers to locations, ensuring that they had the necessary travel documents, and obtain permission to film in each country. While I had been a coordinator at a studio and had seen productions at work, this was something very new to me, and I wanted to do everything I could to excel, including not making any mistakes. I wanted to look like I knew my stuff at all times.

Trying really hard to act like I knew something was my first mistake.

Just after I was hired, Bert was going on a trip to look at the various locations where we were planning to film as well as meet the local facilitators who would assist us. He gave me his plan, "Can you put together an itinerary for Johannesburg, Nairobi, and Dar Es Salaam? We'll book Europe later." I told him that it was exciting that he was going to Africa and India. This was my effort at trying to bond with him by showing off my knowledge of the world.

"What!?" he replied.

"Dar Es Salaam, in India, pretty cool." I said smiling, hopeful that we were sharing a bonding moment.

"That's in Tanzania," he replied, looking rather annoyed as he walked out of the room.

Oops. I pledged then and there not to open my mouth about a place until I knew where it was. And where on earth was Tanzania, anyway? Well, it was in Africa. I realized that there were more places in Africa than just the Congo. I felt downright stupid. I had never taken geography. I could tell you anything about tectonic plates, having taken geology, so knowing where countries were was something I had to quickly learn. We weren't wired for the internet just yet, so I had to go old-school and got a couple of maps and books on travel. I also got a small pocket atlas so that I wouldn't have a "geographical malfunction" again. I didn't want to send Bert somewhere other than where he planned on going.

One thing I did learn while working at a studio was that every first season of any show is the absolute worst and hardest to do. Every show I had seen ramp up for the studio always had a heavy turnover of staff after the first season because of various problems that had cropped up. Even though schedules and plans looked great on paper, you have to go through at least one season to see how a production will really work. Looking back, it's amazing how we pulled off the first season of *Wild Things* at all.

Starting a show is like reinventing the wheel. Even though you hire people with experience on other shows, people who know what they're doing and how to put a show together, it's still a different animal each time. There is no one way to construct a show because the studios and the networks all have different guidelines and standards to abide by to ensure safety, delivery, and airdates. Even job definitions are different. I've been a production manager on a few shows, but could've just as easily been called a production coordinator or even a line producer or executive in charge. While there are some things that I always do as a production manager, there are many other tasks that vary from show to show, depending on how the show is structured and what your boss expects of you. Sometimes I was more of a production coordinator than a production manager, and other times I was more of a line producer than a production manager. Whatever my title, it was my goal to do as much as possible, learn as much as possible, and, most importantly, become irreplaceable.

The first season of a show is also the first time the staff gets together, builds an entire infrastructure of crew, contacts, and stories that come together to make the show work. In other words, it's like putting a multi-million dollar company together in a matter of weeks that is expected to run smoothly and stay within a pre-determined budget for a short amount of time. We figure out what stories we're going to tell, how we're going to tell them, and when we're going to tell them. All of that ends up on a shooting schedule that looks good on paper. Everyone agrees it can be done, and then we start filming.

As soon as the initial schedule is on paper, it changes completely.

During the first season of *Wild Things*, the production was flipped upside down a number of times. We would need to reschedule the flights and crew and interview subjects to make the new schedule work. Not because mistakes were made, but because what was envisioned wasn't exactly going well, the studio didn't like a story, it was the wrong time of year to film a particular animal, or our on-camera personality was not available. There were any number of reasons why the schedule might be changed. And this was the sort of thing that happened daily. Everything was in flux up until the moment the crew left for a country. Even then things would change. And without the creativity of the producers in the field, there would have been no show. They would change stories on the fly, getting some great, unexpected shots. So the people in the field had to change how they worked, and those of us at the main production office a couple of continents away would have to change how we worked with our overseas counterparts to make sure that what was shot made it to air. There were even some stories that were filmed that didn't end up airing for one reason or another. Stories weren't as interesting as had initially been thought, the wildlife was hard to capture on camera, or the studio hadn't liked the story. Still, even with all this apparent chaos, we were able to make great television. If it had been any other "normal" company, it wouldn't have survived.

One day the production manager, my boss, finally decided to go out to lunch, which was very, very rare. She had just finished a meeting, and we now had the list of countries and places we were planning to use for the show. I needed to start putting together travel arrangements and research how to go about getting permission to film in those countries but by the time the production manager returned an hour later, everything had completely changed at least twice. She swore she would never go out to lunch again.

First seasons are the most stressful of any time on a production because there is a battle for getting the show shot and "in the can" and getting it to air. And with everything up in the air and constantly changing, the pressure rolls downhill right into the laps of those who can do little or nothing without their supervisor's help. There isn't a moment of peace. When I worked as a coordinator for a large studio, I would see a high percentage of crew members leave after the first season on scripted shows, disheartened and upset about how hard it was to get a show off the ground. It was even more stressful for shows that were unscripted, with a general outline and no exact plan.

The second season staff benefits from the first season's mistakes. The screw ups, the missed shots, the overtime, the unknown costs that would cause the studio headaches would be worked out as the staff reviewed the mistakes made on the first season. The first season is about education, dedication, and determination. And I needed all three of those qualities to succeed in the first season of *Wild Things*. I needed to be educated about the world, I needed to dedicate my time to figuring out the problems, and I was determined to stay for further seasons.

I also formed a very bad habit at that time.

I decided to eat, breathe, and live the show. I believed that I should be the only one who could solve problems, and I didn't want to give anyone else the chance (What an ego, right?!). I took my job way too personally, to the point of foregoing any personal life. I decided early on that I would handle whatever came my way. I would take whatever was wrong and lay it squarely on my own shoulders. If something fell apart, it was my fault. If I tried to fix something and couldn't, it was my fault. If something happened that wasn't my fault, it was my fault for not stopping it before it happened. I wanted to be the lightning rod for problems, assuming all the responsibility of failure. Well, that was pretty unintelligent, but at the time I rationalized it by telling myself that I needed to make sure everything ran smoothly so that my bosses could be free to be creative and those around me could be free to do their work better. I needed to prove to myself and others that I could handle the pressure.

By the end of the first season, I had been promoted to production manager and was working directly with crews in South Africa, India, and Australia… basically all the countries where the time difference was so great that I had to get up in the middle of the night to make phone calls.

The show was a huge production. It involved researchers, story editors, field producers, editors, fixers, and camera crews all over the world, not to mention all the storytellers, the various facilitators in countries we were visiting, and the studio. And we had tight deadlines. There were deadlines to finish shooting, deadlines to finish cutting the shows, and deadlines to air the shows. This was a big undertaking and could be overwhelming. But I was able to learn many new things and help define my roll on the show; it gave me the chance to stretch my professional muscles. The fact that the show was so complicated meant that each day was a huge adrenaline rush. There was always something new to figure out, a country to research, travel to change…never a dull moment. I also got to see how everyone else handled the "excitement" of a difficult show with crazy deadlines and situations.

As I got used to working with Bert, like any boss, I got into a routine with him. There were three things I learned while working for him that can be true of any executive producer.

#1. There was never anything wrong with his equipment.

Besides brushing up on geography, the other big thing I needed to learn about was equipment—cameras, lenses and audio. I had to know who needed what type of camera and audio equipment and where I could rent it from. Two of the cameras were Bert's, and I had to use them for three years and they were much older and had seen a lot of videotape.

I don't know if it was the cameras or the people or a little of both. But I never had a moment's peace with Bert's cameras. Something was broken, something needed to be replaced. The batteries were so old; they could not hold a charge. I had the batteries secretly tested because I needed to prove to him that they needed to be replaced. Some didn't last ten seconds; others lasted between one to five minutes. He still wouldn't budge on buying new ones. The crews were allowed to take three batteries and he didn't want to hear that there was a problem. Well, I sure heard about it. Some of the cameramen used to complain on videotape right before the batteries went out. I would have crews coming back furious, telling me they'd needed to use a car battery attached to the cameras to be able to shoot. And it was certainly a dangerous thing for them to have to do. Bert told me that if he could use his cameras in the field, then the other crews could too. I never fully understood or appreciated what the crews were going through, but I had compassion for their dilemma. It fell to me to try and fix the problem amicably.

I was between two rocks—the rock of the crew who were suffering terribly and not being properly equipped, and the rock of the producer who wouldn't budge. I wanted to fix the problem and also make sure that I was supporting the executive producer and not doing something behind his back that would bite me in the ass later.

So I contacted a camera battery company directly and pleaded with them to give me a good deal on their batteries. They agreed, so long as I was willing to exchange the new batteries for the old ones. I don't remember how I did it, but I presented the idea to Bert and emphasized the cheap price of the batteries and the fact that the production would pay for it. The most important part of that sentence was "the production would pay for it." I don't know if we did, but he went for it. I was very happy. I had won a small battle in what felt like a very long war. And I learned that my job would forever be between two heavily leaning rocks.

#2. Travel never went smoothly for the executive producer.

The first season, I was responsible for arranging the travel plans for everyone on the show, including Bert. He would travel several times during the shooting of a season to make sure things were going okay or to check out a country to see if it was where he wanted to go. But I believe he played a game of dodge ball with the drivers who were assigned to pick him up. If we had a driver picking him up from the airport, we would be on the phone with the driver, who was standing along with the other drivers waiting for people. The driver would never see Bert get off the plane. And then there were times when he didn't get the seats he wanted or the flight he wanted. Things I couldn't necessarily control, but they always put him in an ugly mindset. He'd get into a chronic bad mood after traveling. And I'm sure he thought I was personally responsible.

#3: Every morning Bert needed to have a "screaming" moment.

Not a high-pitched screaming and yell fest with finger pointing and threats, but a recounting of all the problems of the previous day's shooting, his frustrations, and the list of people he didn't like or wanted fired. While he wasn't yelling at me, in particular, I took it personally at first, as if I'd failed to intercede to solve the problem. But after a while, I realized he was yelling through me. And I think a lot of his attitude sprung from the pressure he felt to make sure the show was a success. He just needed someone to listen to all the things he couldn't say to people. He never wanted to be seen as the bad guy. He was always positive and upbeat with his colleagues, no matter how much he liked or disliked them. But I also have to say, in fairness to him, that his yell fests weren't always as impotent as they seemed. He really wanted certain things changed, and I gave him my support, making whatever improvements I could. I always let Mark know when I didn't do something that Bert wanted so that he could help with any damage control.

I had some of my strangest conversations while working on *Wild Things*. I'll never forget a call I got early one morning from a sound person who told me that a gorilla had taken the boom pole (a long pole that the microphone would be attached to so that we could get sound that was farther away from the camera) that had been left outside his sleeping area somewhere in Africa. Another day I received news that a small camera had been killed by a lion. The crew had put a DV camera on top of a remote control car, and then they'd sent the car with the camera on top of it toward a few lion cubs that were playing with each other. The cubs became curious and started sniffing and toying with the camera. While the camera was getting great shots of the baby cubs, it suddenly went dead because the mother, detecting it as a possible threat to her young ones, had decided to chew it to death.

Sometimes I would get a call from the field producer that the government of whatever country we were filming in wanted some outrageous sum of money to release our equipment from customs. I remember fifty thousand being demanded one time. We never paid fifty thousand dollars, more like three thousand dollars. But the absolute worst of the worst was when I had to let the producers know that the animals weren't "performing" on schedule. I had a crew wait for several days on the plains of Africa for the wildebeest to cross a river so we could see the excitement of their crossing. The poor wildebeest would be food for the crocodiles that were lying in wait in the river, so it took a while for them to arrive. And time always cost money and delays. Even though we were documenting what was happening naturally, it had to work with our time frame for filming. And I would say about ninety percent of the time that worked.

Many of these calls would arrive in the middle of the night owing to the time difference. If there were problems at 3:00 a.m. that needed solving at that moment, I had to fix them without anyone else's guidance or help. I could never get any executives on the phone that late at night. So I always dreaded having to come in and tell Bert and Mark the problems that had occurred while they were sleeping—whether it was an animal attack on our equipment or our equipment being confiscated.

I couldn't imagine what it was like to pick up an irate call from our office on the other side of the world. I imagined that they got less sleep than I did. Being in the field was really hard work, and when you don't have a script and can't guarantee that there will be any interesting action, it's almost impossible to give the producers what they want.

The hours were pretty long the first season as I was trying to figure things out, and I was hoping that by the second season it would be easier. I was wrong. For three years on the project, my typical day would involve working at the office for about ten hours, going home, taking a nap for a couple of hours and then working from about midnight to 4:00 a.m., communicating with people in other countries, take another nap and then head into the office early to get out any paperwork that I needed to finish by the end of the day so that I wouldn't miss any deadlines for shooting. I used to keep a pillow and a small television under my desk so I would catch the occasional cat nap at lunch time.

Bert hated that pillow under my desk. I also found out he didn't much care for me, either. The third season of the show, which was also the last, was the hardest for me. The lack of sleep, of a personal life, or anything other than work was taking its toll on me both physically and mentally. My back was hurting because I had a disk that was not in good shape; I had gained weight because I wasn't taking good care of myself; and I started to get snippy and illogical. Even though I tried to put on a funny face and goof off from time to time, in hindsight, I could see that I was getting bitter.

And I did lose it. A few times over the course of that last season Mark told me that Bert wanted me fired. He didn't like me and wanted me out. Mark told me this because he was tired of hearing it from Bert. But it took a serious toll on me. I was feeling insecure; after all, I was doing my job, right? Wouldn't I be fired if I were doing it poorly? I could itemize in my head everything that had gone wrong, everything Bert had complained about, and everything I'd tried to do. My dedication and the long hours I put in meant nothing to Bert. That's what I was thinking. I didn't confront Bert until Mark passed along another fine piece of information. Bert thought I was sharing confidential information with another producer, one who wasn't on our show, and that I was on some sort of "gossip" list.

That last accusation was infuriating. Bert was talking about a former producer on the show who was supposedly getting confidential information from me about our show. He had already worked on the show previously so I couldn't have revealed anything that he didn't already know. And the only time I had spoken to this producer was to recommend a friend for a job. She had worked with him for a few years, but while I was working at *Wild Things*, my friend and I barely spoke, mostly because I had wanted to avoid being accused of giving away private information to her, which is exactly what Bert thought was happening anyway. Knowing how paranoid Bert could be, I had sacrificed a friendship to allay his fears which was futile. When Mark told me this, I immediately barged into Bert's office, mad as hell.

He was in a good mood that day. Everything was going well. After three years, we had all fallen into some sort of routine, and the filming was going smoothly. It was toward the end of the final season, and I think he was looking forward to taking a break or doing another show. But I was quick to ruin his good mood.

"I hear I'm on some list?" I told him. He was shocked. I recounted the story that Mark had told me, and I said, "I've lost a friendship because I've tried to make sure that I did nothing that would upset you, so whatever list I'm on, remove me, immediately. It's wrong and I won't stand for it."

He assured me that I had nothing to worry about, that I was definitely not on some list. I walked away, happy that I'd said something but annoyed that he hadn't owned up to what he'd told Mark. I felt like I had just burned a bridge.

CHAPTER 2
NOT ONLY AMAZING, BUT A MIRACLE

Even though there were a lot of shaky moments, hot heads, screaming sessions, equipment failures, lack of sleep, and the occasional vendetta, *Wild Things* was a great experience. I learned so much about the world and made some incredible, long-lasting friendships. The job gave me the chance to become an integral part of an international show and learn a great deal about getting into countries, dealing with political systems, and calculating exchange rates.

I was now hooked on the reality production drug.

I'm still a user. It's a highly addictive and intoxicating drug, with tremendous highs and horrible lows. I am on a high when I'm in the middle of chaos; fixing problems, trying to manage budgets, huge mishaps, and anything else that might come my way. I think of it as slaying a dragon. It's a total adrenaline rush. The tremendous lows come when nothing is happening. When you're too exhausted to think or when you aren't able to fix the problem. The lows are incredibly frustrating because you want to be in that rush, but something's blocking your way, as if a policeman has pulled you over for going 100 mph in a 30 mph zone. Nothing is worse than not being able to solve a large problem and having to walk into your boss's office with bad news. Then everything calms down and the cycle begins again.

It was truly exciting to be up all night fixing things, and then come into the office to work on the next shoot and solve emergencies. There is a rush in solving problems and overcoming stressful situations that gives you a real boost of confidence and accomplishment. So it was sad when the show ended, but we had heard that there was only going to be three seasons, so it wasn't a shock.

Once the show was over, it felt like I had finished a sprint. I was tired, but I wanted to run another race. It was such a great and challenging experience, and I knew nothing would ever compare to it. Regardless of my relationship with Bert, I was truly going to miss working on his show. His vision and his excitement had made *Wild Things* great, and I enjoyed buying into the whole package. And even though he had supposedly wanted me fired, I was the only original production person who had remained on the show for all three seasons, so that had to mean something. To this day, I keep in touch with many of my colleagues from the show, and it's cool to see their names on other shows, or to see them grow in their own careers as producers or storytellers.

After the show ended, I started to look for work again, something I hadn't done in three years. It was incredibly different. I did land a couple of jobs, but they didn't compare. The production drug wasn't the same; it wasn't working. The problems were not as complicated and it seemed almost too easy to work on anything else. I realized that *Wild Things* wasn't going to be replicated in terms of the adrenaline rush. I needed to kick the drug or find a different kind of challenge.

A few months had passed, and then I received a call out of the blue. Imagine my surprise when Bert was on the other end of the line. I was shocked!

He was very jovial, joking and talking about a show he was going to do. He said he was looking to put some of the old gang back together. I told him that I was working, but that I'd be happy to speak to him as the show came together. It was a great conversation! And I was flattered that he had actually called me. Of course I thought about the conversation way too much, and analyzed the five-minute phone call over and over. I felt that all the work I had put into *Wild Things* was now positively justified, that he really did like me and appreciate my work, and that perhaps Mark had been playing some sort of bizarre practical joke on me. Since I hadn't ever heard Bert tell me he wanted me fired or didn't like me, then he must actually like and respect me, right? The call made my day, and I had to call Laura, the accountant on *Wild Things*, and let her know.

In the meantime, I stayed where I was and continued to build the staff. One position I had to hire was an editor. And as things go, I looked for recommendations. The one person who kept coming up was someone I'd worked with on *Wild Things*, Eli.

I ended up hiring him—he was funny and personable and a great fit for the position. Unfortunately, the show made some stylistic changes, and I bowed out because I felt that it would be better served by a producer who had more experience with films and commercials. So I left after staffing the show with many of my wildlife show colleagues. I don't believe in hanging around if you don't think you have the resources to do a good job. I didn't have another job to go to, so I wasn't jumping ship for a better gig, I just didn't want to do something for several months that was so out of my league. I felt that it was the best thing for me and for the show. But I was satisfied to know that I'd left it in good hands, and that the staff I had assembled would do a good job.

While I was looking for another job, I got a call from Bert again. This time he wanted to meet with me. This was very well timed. His office was in a really cool building that's hidden away on the west side of Los Angeles, in a place you wouldn't think a really cool building would be. It was impressive. I did the usual interview things—I dressed up, arrived ten minutes early, and waited for a few minutes. I was playing the getting-a-job game. I figured that I had a good shot since I had already worked with Bert. He explained that it would be an international race around the world, and it sounded very exciting. It tapped into my desire to be on another crazy international show.

I figured that there would be more money since it was a network show, so I wanted to see about negotiating a better deal. The only time I'd ever made a play for more money was with *Wild Things*. I was a lousy negotiator for myself, and I pretty much took what was offered for a lot of reasons—I didn't have enough experience to garner more money; I was convinced the production company didn't have enough in their budget to afford me; and I was never in a position *not* to take a job. I was afraid that if I turned down work or stood my ground, I'd be unemployed, and I didn't have enough money stashed away for that eventuality. Essentially I am the first person in line to shoot myself in the foot. No one else needs to do it for me.

Finally Bert's assistant took me upstairs to the conference room. Then Bert told me about his show. It was international, a lot of the same people would be working on it, and it was confidential. Again, I was swept away by the grandness of his vision. The show would be structured very much like *Wild Things* in terms of crew, countries, and travel. I totally wanted to do it. I could tell that I would be back among friends in a challenging, thrill-a-minute environment, and I couldn't ask for anything more. I would be back on the production drug in no time, solving problems and making the impossible possible.

While regaling me with all the possibilities of the show, he threw a zinger in the middle of his monologue. I didn't realize it until after the interview, and even then I dismissed it, but the sentence would come back to haunt me. He said, "All of this needs to be confidential. **I know how you can talk…**"

There it was, the zinger. I thought nothing of it, except that his idea was very hush-hush, and he didn't want anyone to hear about it. I said, "No problem." He thanked me for coming, and told me he'd be in touch. When I was driving home, that last strange line ran through my head a few times, but I let it go.

I didn't hear back from Bert or his assistant.

I did hear from Terry, the new guy, who happened to be the executive in charge. I did not know him, but I had heard of him, as he'd worked on another show across the street from *Wild Things*. I would often go over to the set where he worked and played an after-hours poker game with some of the staff on his show. I knew he had been a production manager, so the fact that he was an exec in charge now meant that he'd made the step up. My connections told me that he'd been recommended by another friend and was very good to work with. I met with him, but before we could speak to each other, I had to sign a confidentiality agreement pledging not to discuss the show with anyone. We proceeded to have a very weird conversation. I found out that he had already hired another production manager and quite a few other people. And then I was smacked with another zinger, quite similar to the first.

"I hear two things about you. That you are great and I should hire you, **but the negative is that I know how you talk about your crew."**

That was a hit out of left field that I hadn't been expecting. How I talk about my crew? Hmmmm. He was hesitant to hire me for that reason. I could only respond with something like, "I'm not sure what you mean, but if you mean that I openly assessed the abilities of the crew of *Wild Things* and spoke frankly with the executive producer, my other boss, and the other production managers, then that would be true. But anything that was ever discussed about a crew member, I was sure to say to him or her as well, so I didn't go behind anyone's back… If that's what you're talking about." I was completely honest with people about why they weren't coming back or what problems were going on, whether it was a personality issue or something else.

I felt that there had to be a lot of conversations going on about me behind my back, and I was trying to figure out why. I met with Bert figuring that I had the job because he was the guy in charge. After all, he was the executive producer, and clearly (in my mind) he had recommended me. Now I was being considered for the second production manager position, and it seemed as though Bert wanted Terry to choose his own team. So my hopes of having a leg up were dashed. I wasn't quite sure what to expect anymore.

I was also afraid that I wasn't even going to be a production manager. Though I was being interviewed for a position *titled* Production Manager, the job description seemed to be more in line with a travel coordinator. I told Terry my rate, which he said was too high. He told me that I would have to come down a bit if I wanted the job. I agreed, figuring that one season on this high profile show would be good experience for me. At this point, the game had changed for me. I was no longer the "Diva of Production."

And then he told me that he'd hired Philip, whom I knew from *Wild Things*, as a production manager who was on the show for only a few months as we wrapped up season one.

Oh man, that was the best news I could have heard. If I had to be second banana to anyone, it would be Philip. When I worked with him on *Wild Things*, we had a great time. Everyone liked Philip because he was easy to get along with and had high standards and a good sense of humor. We were always kidding around with each other with verbal sparring and trying to one-up each other. I'd work with him again in a heartbeat.

Even with Philip on board, it was definitely a blow to find out that there were two Production Managers, and I was the afterthought. Stupid, ego-driven thoughts started to whizz through my head. The sort of self-destructive mental talk that could ruin a person's career was exactly what I didn't need at this point. Basically, I was thinking that I should've been picked first, after all I was the EP's choice, and I deserved at least some kudos for years of loyalty on the job. As quickly as I had these thoughts, I shrugged them off, knowing that Philip and I respected each other, and would enjoy working together.

I lit up and said, "He's great. I love him, and can't wait to work with him!" Terry looked puzzled by my response, and then pleased. Even so, I still wasn't sure I was going to get the job. I left the interview befuddled and disappointed.

But I got the call about a couple of weeks later. The job was mine if I wanted it.

I was excited. I didn't care I was making a little less than I wanted. I was going to work with many of the same people from *Wild Things*. I believed that I was going to experience the same euphoric and tough schedule that I'd had the last time I worked on a show for Bert, and that this show would be just as memorable as the first.

A couple of people that I had been in touch with knew that I was on the show, and they asked me to put their names up. I did, and it felt good that they were hired. Eli happened to be one of them and I was thrilled that he'd be working on the show. Everything seemed to be falling into place. Philip was living overseas at the time and was moving back to the States to work on *Amazing Race*. So to see him again was wonderful. It was like old times.

Kind of…

This show was a prime-time network show. This was the big time. That meant a lot to me. I had always wanted to work on a network show, but I'd never thought it would be a reality show. I'd assumed I would end up on a one-hour drama series that would be successful for the next ten years. While *Amazing Race* was similar to *Wild Things*, it was even bigger in scope in many ways. It involved more money, tighter deadlines, and contestants.

I had never worked with contestants before. My new job had two parts; I would be working with both the casting department and the production department. I considered myself the coordinator for the casting department because I organized their travel and the travel of the contestants, and was responsible for putting up the casting and semi-finalists contestants at a hotel in Los Angeles. I also had to set up contestant interviews, medical exams, psychological testing, and make sure they'd filled out all their paperwork and turned over their passports. It seemed like a lot for the contestants to go through, but for a pile of money, what did they have to lose?

While I was organizing crew visas, travel, and working with the casting department on travel for them and contestants, Philip was organizing the hiring of the crew and equipment that we needed and arranging for it to be shipped. The production managing part of the job was very big, and I was grateful that both Philip and I were on board. One person could not have done everything that was required that first season. Normally, for a smaller show you have a production manager, and then a production coordinator below them. We had no coordinator on the show, so I saw myself as the production manager-coordinator. A hybrid with enough work for two people.

I settled into the enormity of my job. The work I needed to do for the crew was fairly straightforward because I only had to get them the visas they needed for the trip and I was hoping to get the contestants additional visas in their passports so that they wouldn't necessarily know where they were going. But I had one problem in getting the visas;

We didn't know where we were going.

The details for the show were changing all the time, and nothing was set in stone. And to get visas for around forty crew members plus twenty-two contestants, I needed time. So I decided to cover my bases and tried to get visas for the cast and crew of any and all countries that were mentioned. Of about

400 countries, around 150 required visas. I made a point of keeping track of all the countries and the paperwork they required on a spreadsheet. While I wasn't sure exactly where we were going on the show, it was easy to surmise which countries we were most likely to visit, since it would be easier to utilize the previous contacts and facilitators we'd used over the three years of *Wild Things*. At least that's what I figured, which helped narrow down my workload quite a bit.

My production drug was on overload. I'd never been so busy. The whole staff was buzzing. There was so much to complete in such a short time. I felt that I had hit my professional stride. I was working on something that was challenging but manageable. While in the past I had constantly second-guessed myself, now I had confidence. I knew what I was doing, and it was like riding a bike downhill. Even though I had done this sort of work before, I'd never done it within such a small window of time, especially given the reality that the show was still in flux, and things were changing as the producers traveled around the world to see if what we were attempting to do would work. There were changes right up to the last minute. And changes on an international show can be very hard to quickly facilitate.

There was a "war room" where the producers would work out the logistics, games, and rules of the show. It was a room with a large map on one wall and schedules and ideas on another, and it was exactly how I imagined a room in which generals would arrange a military operation. The producers would go through the entire world, coming up with ideas and trying to plot out various places to go and the order to go in. I'm betting that these guys could run a small country. I am always in awe of the producers and all the ideas they would come up with. There is always a lot of arguing, what was good and not good. And mostly I remember a lot of laughing. After all, they were creating the show from scratch and really had to envision how things would actually run on the race. They would need to have some kind of ESP to figure out all the angles of what could happen in a country. The reality is you can't figure out everything, but you can sure try.

By the time I started on *Amazing Race*, *Real World* had been on for almost a decade, and *Survivor* and *Big Brother* had already been on for at least one season each. So people were just getting used to the larger competition shows, but there was nothing as big in scope or as complicated as *Amazing Race*. And the running around the world, well, that was the biggest challenge of all. So it felt like I was a part of something really groundbreaking. Aside from the responsibilities I had on *Wild Things*, I was also responsible for working with the casting department. I wasn't quite sure what to do with them, but the one big rule I tried to remember was, "Just ask everyone what you can do for them." And as people tell you what they need, you figure out what you are doing. I never had any sort of official outline of what my job responsibilities were, except that I was supposed to do what I had always done.

As soon as you walked into the office, there was a large bullpen, an area with tables, phones and computers, and then there were little offices along the walls. I set up shop in the bullpen, so I got to see everything that was going on around me. The mood was exciting and frenetic. The funniest part was watching videotapes of potential contestants talking about why they should be on the show. Some were absolutely hilarious. In one of them, a naked woman was dancing with her two little Chihuahuas covering her breasts. I wasn't quite sure why that would've made her a great contestant. Then there were people singing or dancing in their pleas to be on the show. And there were also a few really boring ones. I think there should be a show about all the audition tapes or, at the very least, a dedicated YouTube category. At the time, I didn't realize that the best contestants might not always be the most normal. My version of a "best contestant" was someone who knew the world, had the athleticism to power through all the demands of the events and was able to run to the finish line. But it was much more—or *less*—than that. The contestants needed to be entertaining while also being physically equipped to meet the show's challenges. They had to have that "IT" factor, like the actors who were cast on regular scripted shows.

There were hundreds of tapes that the casting people were going through, but they finally managed to narrow it down to the semi-finalists who would be seen by the producers and then the network. These people would come to Los Angeles for interviews, fill out a barrage of forms, and undergo testing. I moved from the production office to the nearby hotel where the semi-finalists were staying, and I set up an office in one of the hotel rooms. I had a suite with a bedroom in the back and an office area up front. I had my computer set up, and I was ready to go. I was sort of a babysitter for the potential contestants. If they needed something or had any questions, they'd come see me in my room. I would also have them wait there before going to see the producers or doctors. I got to know quite a few of them pretty well. I became a den mother to them.

While I was at the hotel, I was still working on visas for the crews as well as getting all the paperwork settled for the contestants. I had the latest versions of what countries they'd be visiting. So while I spent my days with the contestants, I had to make sure that no one went and peeked at what I was doing. So whenever anyone came into the room, I'd pop up a Valentine's Day card on my computer screen. I'd pretend to be working on the card while the contestants were in my room. I came up with some sort of crazy story about a make-believe boyfriend. When the contestants left my room, I went back to working on the visas. I had to make phone calls and send out e-mails, but most of the work needed to be done either late at night or early in the morning. Still, I didn't feel like I was getting enough done during the day, the contestants were coming and going all the time, interrupting the flow of my work.

There were some interesting contestants who liked to "stir the pot," as it were, and they made the job a lot more interesting.

There were two girls from Texas who were particularly fond of causing trouble. It was quite hard to keep them in their room or even keep track of them. One day, they came into my suite with a desk bell. They told me they'd gotten it from the Bell

Captain, and I should ring it so that the contestants could hear me when I needed them. I had to laugh, but I returned it to the front desk immediately. One time they had a night off, and they decided to go out and have some fun. They saw me, jumped into my convertible and I dropped them off at a restaurant where they were going to meet some people. They were quite the party girls and were raring to cause some trouble with their smiles. I was just trying to stay neutral.

There were another couple of guys who were quite the opposite. They would sit in the lobby and take notes. Just sit and take notes all day. I could see them from outside my room. They would wave at me, pads in hand. They would watch the producers sometimes, but they mostly paid attention to the other contestants. One morning they commented on how nice I looked in my car and what I was wearing and where they thought I was going. If I hadn't known they were incredibly nice, I would have thought they were kind of creepy. They were starting to play the race before they were even in it. They liked visiting my room as well. I always worried that they'd find a way to see what was on my computer, that I wasn't as savvy with them as I should have been. But if they knew something they shouldn't have, they never said anything to give it away.

It was hard to be away from the office for so long. As I've mentioned, Philip was starting to get the crew together and the equipment ordered, so we needed to be in contact with each other to make sure we were in sync with any changes to the race. It became stressful to have the contestants hang out with me all the time. I tried to find ways of getting them out of my room. Sometimes I'd just say, "I have to make a call, so you need to leave my room." I knew they would be standing by the door or nearby, so sometimes I would go to the bedroom to take the call to make sure they didn't hear anything.

I took confidentiality very seriously, and I didn't want to be the person who screwed up the entire show by giving something away. This was the paranoia that stayed with me throughout my experience with *Amazing Race.* I was paranoid I would be solely responsible for the show going into the toilet.

That was my biggest fear.

Well, after interviews and testing, the finalists are finally picked. I had a bunch of forms for them to fill out and sign piles of visa applications, and—for some—passport applications. The two women who liked trouble and the two men who liked note-taking all made it as finalists.

Now it was time for the contestants to have their medical exams and shots and visit the network one last time. They got the standard number of shots that were required while traveling. I say standard, because they were the same ones we'd get for our crews when I was on *Wild Things*. We also gave them medication, if needed, for malaria and a couple of other things that would help them stay healthy on the trip. Malaria pills don't necessarily prevent you from getting malaria, but they sure can give you some crazy dreams. A lot of people don't take it because of the side effects. Everything was running pretty smoothly, except that some of the visas were being processed slowly. The finalists returned home and started to prepare for their trip without knowing where they were heading.

After that, I had more time to focus on the crew.

It was more difficult to get visas for the crew. First of all, they were from all over the world. We had crews from South Africa, Israel, South America, and throughout the U.S. So I had to get visas for some people, and others had to get them on their own, facilitated by a letter from me or an embassy that would help smooth the approval process. Certain crew members needed more visas than others depending on what country they were coming from, which complicated matters. At times like these I wished that we had used crews from one country to make the whole process more efficient. And I also had to apply for different visas for the crew than for the contestants. Contestants would be traveling on visitors' visas, but our crews had equipment and would be filming. In some cases they needed special clearance for that. To help get visas for the crew, we often had to have the facilitator in the country we were visiting provide a letter of invitation to the production company before moving forward. I don't want to make this a lesson in how to get a visa; I just want to make the point that the paperwork and bureaucracy involved in travel were crazy even before 9/11!

And then I got my first heart-stopping shock.

Israelis are not allowed into some countries, period.

I had never heard of this before. I had experience with British passports, which seemed to allow those who held them into every country without a visa—I figured it was because they owned half the world at one time—but I had never heard of anyone not being allowed into a country because of race. The show was going to one country that would not allow in

Israelis. I had to let Bert know about this. He wasn't too happy, but we had to make sure that a couple of our crew members would skip that country, moving ahead to the next one in the race. I never enjoy sharing news like that with a producer because it messes with their plans. I needed to make sure Bert would be reminded of the issue as the race got closer.

On average, I needed three or four visas for each passport for the crew and contestants. Many of the visas took several weeks to acquire. On average, India takes six weeks, and it didn't seem to matter what we did to try and expedite it. The process was long and complicated. We had to send applications to the embassy in Washington, which were approved first in the country, and then in Washington. After that, I had to get all the information to the country's west coast embassy. And the information never seemed to be the same between D.C. and the west coast. So I would have to try three or four times to make sure that the information on the west coast and in D.C. was the same so that I could get the actual visas on the actual passports, and then send the passports to other embassies for approval. I could not do multiple countries at one time. I had to get approval one country at a time for each passport. And I was looking at a calendar every day counting down the days I needed to have all the passports in.

And because it took six weeks to get the visas for India, I was not able to get any "fake" visas for the contestants after all. I wanted to have visas in each contestant passport that would be a rouse so they would not look at their passport and assume they would be going to those countries. Probably smart that I was never able to do that, as I'm sure the countries wouldn't have appreciated it.

Time was not on my side in getting the visas done for the show.

One problem was getting the visas for China. We would have to pick up the visas for China in India while we were running the race. This was cutting it close. I wasn't happy that we wouldn't have them in advance, but I didn't have a choice. So I had all the visas for the contestants that I needed, except China. It made me nervous. I had to rely on the Producer of the China segment to come through. And I'm never comfortable leaving my job in someone else's hands.

The pressure was building as we got closer to the first day of shooting; some things were coming together and some were coming apart.

And then a stupid wrench hit me.

I saw the actual budget.

Laura, had done the initial budget for the show through our production company that we had started to create budgets for film and television. She didn't run the budget by me or even tell me about it; it was all confidential. It was one of the first gigs for our little company. I mostly worked with film people, and she worked with television people. I figured the budget was a lot like a *Wild Things* budget, and I didn't care to see it. But temptation was left out on Bert's desk one day...

The funny thing was that I wasn't even looking at the budget. I was speaking with Bert about visas and updating him on my progress. Bert stepped out of the office for a moment to answer a question. As I sat in front of his desk my eyes swept down for a moment, and I saw the budget, upside down, and I saw a line item. I don't know why it registered with me, but it had a big impact.

I saw what Philip was getting paid...and it was about thirty percent more than what I was getting paid.

I was stunned. Bert returned and we continued our conversation, but I actually stopped listening and went on auto-pilot. I wasn't upset at the time, just stunned and confused. A cold streak ran up my spine.

Now, as I've said, Philip was my friend, and I was a big fan of his. One time while we were working on *Wild Things*, he asked me about my salary. At the time I was a production coordinator and he was a production manager, so I figured it wouldn't be anything close to what he was making. I told him that I didn't feel comfortable discussing my rate. He told me what he made, and I told him that it was better than what I made, but I had always stuck by my hard and fast rule of not comparing salaries. So as soon as I saw that figure on Bert's paperwork, I wished I could unsee it.

It bothered me. There were so many emotions I was experiencing, but it boiled down to this—I felt angry, betrayed, and conned. I tried to justify the difference in our salaries. I came up with some ideas: It shouldn't bother me; after all he was hired first. He had a family, so he needed more money. But then I started thinking, why wasn't *I* hired first? Why hadn't I gotten the preferential treatment and higher pay? After all, I was the one who worked for Bert for three years, edging my way up through the ranks. Why was my friend getting more money than

I was after working on *Wild Things* for only half a season? And why should having a family make it okay for him to get paid more than someone who was single? I couldn't figure out any solid reasons for such a large discrepancy. I was working for two departments, staying later, and doing things that even he told me he couldn't do. When I was on *Wild Things*, I had done all of this too. I could replace him, but he couldn't replace me. Didn't that make me more valuable? And I felt stupid for not fighting more for the money at the outset, but I knew I wouldn't have gotten the job if I had been insistent. I felt discriminated against. And I really started disliking Bert. I couldn't even look at him.

I know people get hired because of who they know, and their salaries were settled in the same way. And I understood that Terry knew Philip before he knew me, and he felt confident that he would do a good job. Philip got a better deal because of his connection. But my connection was to the big cheese, top dog, and it apparently hadn't been enough to garner a prime salary, which seemed a little backwards. But in the back of my mind I knew that Bert needed me more than he liked me. He hadn't been willing to take a stand for me. I was able to bury what I was feeling, since I knew it was moot. No one cared except for me. I decided that

I would only be there for one season, no more, unless I got more money.

The only time the discrepancy ever upset me again was when someone else on the staff needed a raise, and they got it without much fuss. The head honchos hadn't even been willing to give me my measly rate. So my mind went down that negative path again. I had to tuck it away and forget about it for a while, though, because the show was hitting the fan. I also didn't sign my crew deal memo for that reason.

Normally I would sign a deal memo that outlined my job and the agreed-upon rate, and it would lay out potential raises for additional seasons. I didn't want to lock myself into a small raise each season, so I only signed the confidentiality agreement that said something about suing me for 40 million dollars if I gave away the ending before the show aired. But nobody ever insisted that I sign my deal. I gladly would have if I had just been getting started, but not when I was making inroads into my career, particularly not when I was getting so much less than the other production manager.

I never blamed Philip. I blamed myself for being taken.

CHAPTER 3
THE BEGINNING OF A LIFE CHANGING MOMENT

I could blame a lot of people and things for what I was about to go through, but whether it was karma, evil spirits, God, or just plain bad luck, it all began with my landlord, a great guy named Rick.

I actually met Rick through a woman whom I met at a 'tall' club, a dating club for people over six feet tall. I had gone to an event out of curiosity, because it was where my parents had met. I was pretty amazed that the club where mom had met my dad was still around. I had just graduated from college, and was looking for an apartment. Though I didn't meet any interesting men at that particular event, a woman there knew a guy whose mom had just passed away, and he was getting ready to rent out her apartment in Venice Beach. I really wanted to live near the beach, and even though I figured I couldn't afford it, I took a couple of friends to see it. It was a great apartment with a front and back yard as well as a garage. Aside from the fact that it had pea green carpeting and a matching pea green stove and washer/dryer, it was spacious and much nicer than the dorms and apartments I was used to in college. It needed some work, but I knew I wanted it. The place where I was living at the time was a house that had been rented out, bedroom by bedroom. I had to share a bathroom with my neighbor, which also doubled for the kitchen and dishwashing area. So that apartment in Venice Beach was like a mansion. It was perfect. But it was pretty expensive for just me to rent. I didn't have enough money for it because I had just started looking for work and didn't have an income. Still, I had to have the place. I could envision the epic parties I would have and the friends I would entertain there. At the time, that was my barometer for any place I looked at. Was it big enough to entertain friends? It was.

There were three bedrooms, so I immediately got two roommates. I advertised in the local paper, and the first two people who responded were my first two roommates.

I did use that apartment to its fullest for about fifteen years. I had monthly poker parties, and Christmas, Thanksgiving, and Easter dinners with friends. I even had casino night parties that would kick off the Christmas season. Casino nights were always my friends' favorite party of the year. I would have blackjack tables, craps, and roulette as well as Pai Gow. Everyone would receive ten thousand dollars of Monopoly money to play with. In the end, there were winners and losers, but everyone walked away with some sort of prize or party favor. I enjoyed doing all the cooking and preparing for these parties. I felt like I was living my poor, urban version of *The Great Gatsby*. I also loved being close to the beach, and would take evening walks to look at the beautiful homes and meet some wonderful people who lived in the neighborhood. I started to make roots and figured that I'd found the place I'd be for the rest of my life. Maybe not in that apartment, but somewhere in Venice Beach.

Rick, my landlord, was a wonderful man. He let me do anything I wanted in my apartment, from painting to buying new appliances. We didn't see each other often, but we did have great conversations every now and again for a couple of hours at a time. He would put on a picnic once a year and I would get a chance to visit with him and his friends. He was a school teacher, very funny and just about the most honorable guy you could ever meet. He raised my rent only once in fifteen years, and he didn't care that I'd had about twenty roommates over that period of time (another story for another time). I paid on time, took care of my place, and made sure he was informed of any problems. He didn't need to even come down to look at the apartment, because I made sure to take care of everything. I lived in the apartment below, and there was another tenant above me who had been there for a very long time as well. And compared to elsewhere in the neighborhood, our rent was incredibly low. Rick told me that he didn't care about raising rent; it was more important to him to have good tenants. He also knew that I wasn't making a lot of money, so he didn't want to jack up the rates so much that I'd have to move out. He only had three tenants in that duplex in his entire life. I used to joke with him about getting his will done and making sure that I'd get the place when he passed on because I had been there the longest. Well, it was a valiant effort on my part, suffice it to say. He never had a will—or at least not one that could be found.

The last year that Rick was alive we had only a handful of conversations. But each time we spoke he would talk about a nagging ear infection that was, I believe, ultimately part of the cause of his death. It was a shock because he wasn't much older than I was, and I'd had no idea that his condition could be fatal. He probably hadn't even known. One of his dearest friends called me to let me know that they had found his body. But they couldn't find a will of any kind in his home. I didn't even think about what that might mean for me. I was too shocked and saddened by the sudden death of a good friend. The impact of this tragic news was interrupted by a more immediate issue.

My car blew up.

I was driving to see Laura, on a sunny Saturday afternoon. I had just purchased a new cell phone, had a new job working on *Amazing Race*, and was feeling pretty good about finally making some financial inroads in my life. I was in the fast lane in my imagination, but I was also in the fast lane on the 405 freeway going about 75 miles per hour, listening to some jazz and enjoying the nice weather. Laura lived pretty far away, so I didn't drive out there often. I only went on weekends because I didn't want to worry about rushing to get home on a work night.

I was in a pretty great mood, when all of a sudden I heard a big bang.

I thought someone had shot at me, and my first reaction was to duck. Then I pushed on the accelerator, but nothing happened except that smoke was starting to pour out of the hood of my car. It didn't even occur to me that the car might've caught on fire. All I could do was coast and hopefully get off the freeway. But there is a cardinal rule of driving in Southern California. If someone is in distress in the fast lane, don't let that person over, but pass them as soon as possible so as not to get stuck behind them. It was very difficult to get four lanes over to get to an exit, but I knew the worst thing that could happen was getting stuck in one of the middle lanes. I had this vision of cars swerving around me on both sides, the drivers flipping me the finger.

I got lucky.

I got all the way over, but I didn't have much speed left. Then I got on the exit, and it was all downhill from there. I breathed a sigh of relief. All I could do was push on the wheel of my car, as if that might help it over the edge. I ended up getting safely off the freeway. A special thanks to St. Michael for that one. Wanting to keep my glass half-full, there were two positive things I could come up with about my car blowing up. One: It was time for another car, as this one was clearly dying. Two: I might just be able to afford said car.

I called Laura after my car blew up and told her that it looked like I wasn't going to be coming over. I wasn't sure what I was going to do. In her usual generous spirit, she suggested that I borrow her Ford Explorer while her husband recuperated from his recent brain tumor surgery. He wasn't supposed to drive for six months or so to make sure he didn't have any seizures. I don't know where I'd be without the help of my friends.

Laura's Explorer had problems.

I had a bit of bad car karma. Thankfully my mechanic bought my clunker of a car for a thousand dollars. It probably wasn't worth that much, but he wanted to fix it up for himself. That was fine; I just wanted to get rid of it. After all, Laura had offered me the use of the Explorer for a couple of months. Well, every time I would use that car, which was mostly for driving to dealerships to look for a new car, it would not start. I always had to call a tow service to get it started. No one could figure out what the problem was because it seemed as though every time a tow person would come, they could start the car without a problem. I also had to replace the tires because around that time there was a recall of Firestone tires. The tires were looking a little ragged and starting to peel, so I got that fixed right away. But the car not starting was a problem. Finally, after a few weeks, a mechanic figured out that the issue was a defective lock on the starter. So, with my friend's permission, I had the thing pulled out of the car. At around that time, her husband was cleared for driving, and I returned the Explorer. I didn't have a car yet, but I felt like I was close.

I was determined to take the time to find the right car; do the research, bone up on how to deal with salesmen, that sort of thing. I had already owned five cars, all used, most of which were clunkers. Two were my parents' cars, which my dad was notorious for not maintaining. There was the car that was so busted I needed to tie its doors together so that they'd stay closed (I loved valet parking that one at Saks Fifth Avenue), the car that I sold for $500 bucks before the ad even came out in Auto Trader, the car that was totaled at a stop light by a driver who rammed his vehicle into mine and didn't have any insurance, the one that was hit by a kid and wasn't worth fixing because its value was nil, and finally the car that blew up. I didn't think I could even get a car, but I really wanted a decent car. I wanted a car that wasn't going to give me any trouble, one that I could have for longer than three years without pouring money into it. And I was making more money than I had before, and that would hopefully be the case for a long time. So I was trying to convince myself that it was time for a new car. And I needed it pretty quickly.

Maybe it was the fact I was about to turn forty, or it could be because I had some money for a change, but I decided to buy a convertible. I went back and forth between new and used. New would be an extravagance and used would be more responsible. But I really wanted a brand new, never-been-owned, awesome vehicle. And then I figured I probably had bad credit and couldn't afford the cost of a new car. I kept going back and forth until I made a deal with myself. I would try and get the car I wanted, and when it ended up being too much money, I'd go directly for plan B. I figured I would end up buying used, but there was no harm in trying to get a new car.

I did some research, found the car I wanted, and there were only three in town. None of them were used. Pressed by the need for a car, I decided to go ahead and take the plunge despite my lingering doubts. I had another girlfriend, Kelly, who was also looking for a car because she hadn't owned one in a long time. So we enlisted a mutual friend, Rhonda, to drive us to the Toyota dealership to see the car I wanted. The plan was for Kelly to check out the used cars. Kelly and Rhonda are my closest friends, and they're always around in a pinch. I don't know what I'd do without either of them, and I knew I needed their help in making this momentous decision.

But Rhonda had to bail on Kelly and me that day.

I no longer had the SUV, so I was riding my bike around. It was fortunate that the production office for the show was only a quarter of a mile away from my apartment, so I could ride my bike to work. In the back of my head I thought that there was a slim chance that I might have to move, given all the hubbub following Rick's death, so getting a car was something that couldn't wait any longer. I called Kelly and told her that I would meet her at the dealership (they were expecting me) and that I was riding my bike down. She said she'd ride her bike too and would meet me there.

It was a perfect California moment: I was riding my bike to the dealership with my helmet on when my cell phone rang. It was the dealer wondering when I would be there. I was a couple of hours late to meet with him. So I was riding my bike and on my cell phone on a beautiful November day to buy a new Toyota Solara convertible. Life couldn't be sweeter.

And what about the dealer? Can you think of a better scenario from his point of view? Two girls riding in to his dealership on bikes? This guy knew he had us at the get go. And of course, it wasn't until after the fact that I realized that I was the perfect candidate for getting a crummy deal.

Another reason I had wanted Kelly with me was that she could be the bad cop. She was a good negotiator, smart, and I figured she could tell me if the deal was crazy or not. I never felt like I could negotiate these sorts of things on my own. I had no confidence, so I brought my more aggressive friend with me.

When we arrived on our bikes, we assumed our tough client attitude and looked at the cars. I took the car I wanted for a test drive, going really fast on the freeway, having a lot of fun. And then we get back to the dealership to talk price. My friend and I looked over some numbers, and I called my financial person.

And then my friend left me to go look at some used cars across the street.

I lost my lifeline. I worked with the guy on the numbers. I knew I needed a car, but I wasn't sure if I wanted to buy or lease. Figuring that I didn't have a good track record of having cars for more than three years, I decided to lease it. Of course, after I signed the papers, I immediately remember EVERY single financial television and radio program host saying that leasing is the worst possible deal. NEVER LEASE A CAR. And then, of course, I shouldn't have closed right away either. I should've waited, let the dealer come to me with another price, acted aloof and disinterested. All of that advice started to come back to me only after I had made the agreement. I don't know if it was buyer's remorse or just plain fear that I had taken on something so expensive. Either way I felt a lead necklace around my neck for a few minutes. But I had taken care of a problem that needed solving. Any other problems that would crop up, I would take one step at a time.

As soon as I had the keys to my new Solara Convertible, the dealership returned our bikes to our apartments so Kelly and I could just drive around. It was a November evening and not very warm, but we still had the top all the way down. We drove up the coast to Malibu, all the time Kelly had the seat as flat as possible so she could look at the sky. We had dinner, but felt that since I had a new car, we needed to drive around Beverly Hills and act cool. It was a great night and I had forgotten, for a few hours, what I had to deal with.

Now that I had a car, I had to focus on what was happening with my apartment and the show.

Since Rick didn't have a will, his estate would go to his next of kin. I spoke to one of the relatives who represented the family. She told me that they would be selling the duplex. I was determined not to leave the apartment; after all, I had lived there fifteen years. I felt like it was a home I already owned. I asked for some time to see if I could come up with what was needed to buy the place. They were kind enough and agreed that I could have a couple of months to try and see what I could do. I had great credit, some debt, and no savings. I would need to raise fifty thousand dollars as a down payment. Any good mortgage deals went out the window since I was trying to buy a building, not just a home. I sent a letter to all of my relatives in California and told them that I was trying to buy the place as not only an investment but a place to live, asking if they would be interested in helping with the down payment. I had a cousin who was willing to cooperate, but I didn't have any numbers to give him, and I felt that I needed more than one person to give me money. So after a couple of months, the family decided to go ahead and put the duplex up for sale. It was a hard day when I saw that "For Sale" sign up on my lawn.

Ugh. Fifteen years in the apartment, and now what? Could I stay? Did I have to move? I did a little research, and there were only three ways that I could be thrown out of and apartment. One of them was if the new owner or one of his or her family members chose to move into the apartment. I felt doomed.

I was very busy on *Amazing Race*, so I wasn't around much. I would see someone every once in a while looking around the building, though, and it took less than a couple of weeks for the building to be sold. I started getting distracted at work because I wasn't sure about where I was going to live or when I would be evicted.

And then the rumors started.

My upstairs neighbor and I heard that a couple of guys had bought the place. They were planning to move into her apartment. My neighbor and I were ready to fight. We weren't sure how, but we decided to make sure they stuck to the letter of the law and gave us as much money as possible for moving.

Feeling certain that we would get evicted, my roommates at the time decided to move out. At that point, I could afford the entire apartment by myself because the new owners could not arbitrarily raise rent. It was low enough that I could afford to live there until I figured something out or managed to buy it from the guys. I was doing everything I could to stay in my place.

Well, it didn't work. The landlords, two brothers, decided to each take an apartment. So both my neighbor and I were evicted. We had thirty days. She found a place down the street right away. I was not as lucky. I didn't take any time off to find a place, but I spent every free hour after work looking for a new place and packing up boxes.

I decided that since I needed to move, I was going to make a clean slate of things. I began to get rid of the stuff I hadn't used or didn't want to keep. I felt that any money I could raise from a yard sale would help defray the costs of moving. I hadn't chosen to start my life over, but I was trying to own it by keeping a glass-half-full attitude. I looked forward to starting fresh, but I wasn't looking forward to paying the current rental prices. My rent had been so low and about half as much as it really should've been. Oh well, moving on…

Kelly came with me on scouting missions all over west Los Angeles area in my new red convertible. I had always loved living on the west side of Los Angeles because it was the best place in terms of driving on those horrible freeways in the morning. So I was determined to stay on the west side. We drove all over Santa Monica and saw a lot of places, but nothing that was interesting or even in my price range. Then we happened upon a place that was being renovated. It was a group of bungalow-like apartments, and there were some workers there who were repairing them. We walked around, and I instantly fell in love. They were bright and airy. We didn't get much information about the owner except that he would be back in a couple of days.

I really wanted to live there. I didn't know when they would be ready, but I certainly hoped it was in the time frame I needed. I decided to write a note to the landlord in case I didn't get to see him when he was on site. I wrote him a long letter outlining my dilemma of needing a new place after fifteen years of living somewhere great, and I asked him to give me a call about renting one of the bungalow units. He did. We met, and I picked an apartment that seemed to have a manageable rent. So now I had a new car and a new, very pretty apartment. I was starting to feel pretty okay about life. But there was another snag.

I had no furniture.

After spending fifteen years in the same place, you would think I would have something to show for it. But all of my roommates always had furniture for the living room, dining room and kitchen, as I let them decorate the shared living spaces and their bedrooms any way they wanted. I never cared what my roommates had and was very happy to accommodate them. Now, though, I was in great need of living room furniture for my new apartment. What little furniture I had was what I called "Early American Yard Sale." It was stuff that had been left behind by roommates or neighbors who had moved. All I really owned was a table, a cheap orange dresser, another dresser that was missing a couple of drawers, and a desk that was starting to fall apart. My bedroom looked like it belonged to a college student. It was as if I had never grown up.

I was forty, and I had the apartment of a sloppy teenage boy.

I knew that my mother had furniture she didn't want, furniture that I had loved over the years. We talked about it, and my mom decided that she would ship out a few pieces, and I would incorporate them into my apartment. I was excited. The furniture my mom was sending me was my grandfather's office furniture from the 1950s. My grandfather had been in the film business; he'd directed documentaries and industrial films, and had at one point helmed his own little studio in Hollywood. So it was part of my history and legacy, which was exciting. My mom just welcomed the opportunity to unload the old furniture and buy new stuff.

While I was dealing with the twin debacles of my car and my apartment, I was still working on *Amazing Race*. I would work during the day and at night I would pack and price the items I was selling, look for movers, and organize everything to make the whole transition as smooth as possible, ensuring that it did not interfere with my work. No one at the office knew that I was moving or how much stress I was under.

While I was at the hotel with the semi-finalists, and as my move approached, it was getting harder and harder to part with things. I went into my living room of my soon to be old apartment which had boxes and books and belongings half-organized on the floor. I didn't have furniture, so I had space to spread out. I stared at all of the stuff and started to tear up. I wasn't sad, but I was frustrated. I felt that my life amounted to what was on the floor in the living room, which wasn't much. And some of the stuff had emotional significance or was attached to some fond memory. But it was just stuff. I did not like the fact that I gave everything such significance. After all, my friends, my family, and my work were the things that had true meaning. Not the pile of junk in the room. I was reminded of a time when a couple I knew lost their house to a fire. The years and years worth of stuff they'd collected were destroyed in an instant. And their church threw them a party to begin recouping all they had lost. My job was to buy an iron and ironing board. But there were others who replaced books and clothes that meant something to the couple. As hard as it was for them to lose everything, they chose to look forward, not back. So I rejuvenated myself with the thought that it wasn't over, that the stuff was just that—*stuff.* But no matter what I kept telling myself, it still got to me.

I talked to a couple of friends about how to move into an apartment with as little fuss as possible, but I didn't know how I could pull it off without taking time off from work. They said that I should get some help with the move or tell the show to pay for it, since I didn't have a choice in the matter. I needed to get everything organized without sacrificing my job. I did speak to Terry, and he agreed to help pay for the move, which helped a lot.

My mom was excited. She was finally getting rid of the furniture she'd possessed since she was married and was chomping at the bit to have some newer, nicer things in her home. She had never really liked the furniture, but it was good, solid furniture, and she hadn't wanted to give it away. I think she might have guessed that I would need it sometime down the road—after all, she knew what my old apartment had looked like! She organized a moving company to pick up the furniture in Indiana and deliver it to my new apartment in Santa Monica. Then she would fly out for a visit and help decorate the place and arrange the furniture. She had a good sense of design, so I was looking forward to having her help. Plus, it would be nice to see her.

However I wasn't going to be in town when she arrived.

I had to fly out to New York to start putting things together for the first day of shooting for the very first episode *Amazing Race*. There was a lot to finish. Getting the crew their passports, organizing their flights for them, making sure the hotel was set up, meeting with the New York crew, and helping out with casting when needed. It was quite a busy experience. So when my mom flew in to Los Angeles and started setting up the furniture, I was in New York helping *Amazing Race* get off to a good start. I can't remember how long I was there; I want to say a couple of weeks. But I do know that my hotel room was the production office. We would have meetings with the New York crew there, and I really got to know a few of the crew, especially the production manager, Alison, whom I admired a great deal. She knew her stuff. She rattled off what was needed each day to her crew, and they did what she asked without giving her any guff. She was a real asset, someone I hoped to emulate. She was on top of everything, and she could bark out orders that were followed quickly and efficiently. I couldn't have asked for a better crew.

Everything was abuzz. Network executives had flown into New York, and Philip and Terry were in town too. Philip had his hands full with all the equipment and crew. He set up a ballroom that was filled with gear and organized it for the crew's arrival. I had some last minute problems with visas, and some of the crew had complications with their travel. As the issues mounted, all of us tackled them one by one because we all knew that the show had to go on!

And it did.

That first morning of shooting was exhilarating. We started in Central Park, and I just ran around and did whatever odd jobs needed to be done. My biggest responsibility was to get to JFK and hang out at Al Italia with a flag, indicating to the contestants that they could purchase tickets at that airline to start the race. It was such an adrenaline rush—what we had spent so long preparing for was finally happening—but I was also terrified that something might go horribly wrong. We knew how the show would start in New York City—with the contestants lined up and ready to race—we knew where the contestants needed to go, and we had a good idea of how they would get to the airport. Everything in between was the great unknown. Everything looked good on paper—the route, the tasks the contestants needed to complete, and how the race would end. Easy, right? It was just a race around the world...

On your mark, get set, go!

The show was off and running, and while the contestants were running around like mad people, the crew assigned to follow them were running just as hard. I don't think the audience realizes that when you see a person on camera there are at least two other people following them around—a camera man and a sound man—and they carry about thirty-five pounds of equipment and a small backpack of clothing. So as the contestants were running up the steps from the fountain in Central Park, the crew members were off and running as well. I hopped into a van, and we drove as fast as we could to the airport. We still weren't as fast as the contestants. When we arrived at the airport, contestants were already in line at various airlines trying to get tickets. I was dropped off in just enough time to have my flag sticking out from a column near Al Italia so that they'd see where to go. After all the contestants had bought their tickets, I said goodbye to the camera and sound guys and returned to my hotel room.

It was awesome.

It was kind of a downer to be back in the hotel. Everyone was on a plane to Kenya except for the few of us who needed to wrap up details in New York before returning to Los Angeles. I was already working on the next part of my job, which was anticipating the flight schedules the contestants could take based on where they were supposed to go next. And I was looking forward to seeing how my mom had set everything up in my new home, and just plain looking forward to seeing my mom. As I flew back to Los Angeles, I couldn't help but think that it was going to be great to get settled in my new life and take some time to sort out what I was doing and how all these changes would affect me. I figured I would have some time to adjust.

I never expected what would happen next.

CHAPTER 4
MY DREAM COMES TRUE?

I was really tired. I hadn't been this tired in a long time. The adrenaline rush had completely dissipated, and I was on the plane back to Los Angeles. I was half-awake, a little nauseous, and a little excited- -a complex mixture of feelings wrapped up in one exhausted body. I was looking forward to enjoying some down time now that the race was underway, and I figured I'd have a lot of free time to spend with my mom.

When I arrived back in Los Angeles, my car was waiting for me outside of the arrivals terminal. The top was down, and my friend Kelly was driving. My mom was in the passenger's side. All I could do was cry a little bit (not too much!) and made Kelly get out of the driver's seat so I could drive all of us home.

If I've coveted anything in this life, it's that car. It was my dream car. And I was beyond thrilled to see my mom. She looked great and I was excited to see what she had done with my apartment.

Kelly helped me unload my stuff and took me on a tour of my new place. The two of them had done a better job decorating it than I could ever have done. It looked great. The family furniture that I had loved as a kid looked perfect in my apartment. And the kitchen was all bright with my table and a few knick knacks scattered around. Kelly left, and my mom and I enjoyed some quality time together. We went out to dinner and drove around the city, and then we both got a good night's sleep.

In the morning we went to breakfast at our favorite diner. I was making a list of the places I wanted to take my mom, the relatives we wanted to see, and any movies we needed to catch while she was in town. She hadn't been to Los Angeles in over two years, as she lived in Fort Wayne, Indiana, and the last time we had seen each other was when we went on vacation in Hawaii. I figured it was going to be a great two weeks, and I was happy my mom could spend the time with me.

Our lovely plans were suddenly interrupted.

I received a phone call from Terry in the production office. They needed me on the race. The crew was sick, and things were not going as planned; they needed more help handling the logistics of running around the world. Bert wanted him to go, but his wife was about to have a baby. Philip didn't want to leave his family either. Since I was single and childless, I was the next logical choice. I can't imagine that it sat well with Bert, but I was excited. I was finally going overseas; I could finally use my passport! I wasn't quite sure what my function would be, exactly, but I figured I would see what needed doing when I arrived.

I booked my flight and had six hours left before I got on the plane. I called Kelly again and enlisted her help. I needed her to take care of paying my bills while I was gone. My mom and I stopped by the production office to get some information and the computer programs I would need, and then we spent the next four hours on a whirlwind shopping spree. I had to buy a laptop computer for use on the road and some clothes because I didn't have anything appropriate for the countries we were visiting. I needed shoes that I could use for running around and hiking, and then I had to pack, get some money, and go. Now this was on a Sunday, and since I only had so many hours to pack and get on a plane, I grabbed my credit cards and as much cash as I could so that I wouldn't be caught short on the road. I knew they'd give me a cash advance while I was traveling. Terry was appreciative that I had been willing to leave so last minute.

My mom was very patient as we raced around town preparing for my trip, and Kelly came over to help me pack later on that day. I wanted to take as little as possible, and I decided to take a carry on so that I wouldn't have to check through any luggage. The goal was to be as fast as possible so I wouldn't slow anyone down. I would be gone for about a month, and I figured I wouldn't have time to do laundry, so I bought a lot of underwear and socks that I could throw away instead of washing. I planned on going to every country, so I had to have warm clothes as well as summery ones. My wardrobe was layered to prepare for the changes in weather. But I only had a few outfits because I couldn't take a lot in my suitcase. I also had the computer with me, so I was pretty weighed down for the plane ride.

My poor mom.

After everything she'd done for me, we weren't going to have any quality time together. My mom had about two weeks left at my house. The reality finally hit me, and I felt really bad. I officially hired Kelly to be a step-in daughter to take care of my mom while she was around, and ultimately my mom could stay with our family members for a while before flying back home. I still wanted her to see her family because they didn't go out to see her very often, and it was rare that I would see them unless I took the drive to Orange County. So I was hoping that they would embrace my mom with open arms and that she wouldn't have to spend a lot of lonely days sitting in my home. My mom was very encouraging and never said anything about her situation, which was just like her.

So Kelly and my mom dropped me off at the airport just a couple of days after picking me up there. I had never been to the international terminal before, and it was packed. The lines were huge, and it was more crowded than any domestic terminal I'd ever experienced. I stood in line with my ticket information and my passport. That was when it occurred to me.

I had never traveled overseas before in my entire life.

I'm linguistically challenged, and France—where I was joining the race—was the last place I would've thought to visit. I had always heard that the French weren't very nice to Americans and weren't too tolerant of Americans not speaking their language, so I was not looking forward to that experience.

I started to get that cold feeling through my body that you get when some sort of impending doom is about to strike—when someone menacing is following you or you think you're going to be fired. I had the chills and was nauseous again. I stood in line, and I felt like I looked like some sort of guilty person, that they would figure out that I was some nefarious spy and have me thrown off the flight. For three years, I traveled people all over the world, contacted governments for approval to film, and told crew members how to go through immigration and what to say and do, so I have no idea why these thoughts went through my mind. But crazy scenarios kept traveling through my head like they were on a ticker tape. I think I was paranoid that the years of advice I'd given crew members was about to be proven wrong, and karma was going to come for me like a boomerang. Plus, when rushed, I tend to forget things. So I kept looking at my passport to make sure I hadn't dropped it, and I don't know how many times I checked to see that I had my purse, was carrying the right luggage, and hadn't lost my computer. My senses were heightened, and I'm sure I didn't seem excited to be flying overseas for the first time. I must have looked more like a deer in headlights.

I felt nervous as I approached the counter because I had no idea what I needed to give the agent. I mean, I did know what they needed from me, but I'm sure that I had to be missing some important piece of paperwork. *Oh my god! Would I need a visa?* The thought suddenly occurred to me. *NOW THIS COMES TO MIND???* I had no visas at all for the race, and since I had never traveled overseas before, there was nothing in my passport. I tried to calm myself down. I was going to France first, so I didn't need a visa. Yet. I'd have to pick up any other visas that were needed on the fly. It took about a minute, but the lady at the front gave me my tickets and told me which gate to go to.

Where the heck were the gates? I had never been in the international terminal before, and it was quite a large area. It would be easy to get lost. I just followed some people who weren't going outside.

As I walked past more people, it occurred to me that the international terminal was definitely the melting pot of Los Angeles. I started to relax a bit because I had plenty of time to catch my flight, which gave me time to figure out where I needed to be. I was lost at first, but then I found my way to the right gate. First I had to go through customs. This made me nervous too. Again, I had this irrational, guilty fear that they were going to keep me off the plane for some sort of nefarious evil plan I might've concocted. I tried to dismiss my nerves by telling myself to "shut up and focus." I got through customs okay, but I did have a little scare. They wanted me to start the computer to make sure that it was really a computer. Well, I hadn't charged it up; I had just purchased it, so I wasn't sure it was even going to work. It did. Thank you, Macintosh! Finally, I was through customs and at the gate.

They made our boarding announcement in three different languages, and that was when my weird paranoid scenarios morphed into excitement. This was so cool. How many people got to go overseas for work without having to pay to travel? I was stoked. Remember, this was before 9/11, so things were a little looser and operated differently. I can't imagine doing what I did after 9/11, as the regulations are much stiffer now. If nothing else, I probably looked suspicious. I had done a lot of running around, I'd dropped my bag a couple of times, and I looked a mess. When I got onto the plane and found my seat, I didn't quite fit. It was what my friends call a "cattle" flight. People were squeezed into tiny seats without much leg room. This was a tough one for me because it was a fourteen hour flight, and I'm 6'2" with more leg than body. So I spent the better part of the flight with my knees bulging into the passenger in front of me. I had a lot of time to think on that plane. And then I realized something very important.

What was I supposed to do when I arrived?

Well, that was a question I had quite a few hours to think about. I knew I was going to the hotel to meet up with people, but I just wasn't sure what my role would be. I hadn't been told much about what the problems were. All I knew was that the crew was sick, the events set up throughout the shoot were not as well arranged as everyone had thought, and the race wasn't running as smoothly as it looked on paper. The producers felt that it would be best to have more bodies helping out to make sure everything was in place. Whenever crews are overwhelmed or it seems like there's too much work, people are added to help solve the problem. I'm sure there must have been a great deal of miscommunication. I figured someone would give me more information when I arrived. I landed, got off the plane, and had no idea what to do next. I'm sure I nailed that "deer in headlights" look again.

I couldn't read French. The only language I could speak was English. I had barely made it through Spanish in high school and college. One time I tried taking a semester of Italian at USC, but I didn't last for more than two days. No one spoke English in the class, and when I found out that we were going to be tested on the third day of class, I decided to get out while I still could. I have problems with my own language, let alone another one. But there I was, at the Charles De Gaulle airport, surrounded by French. After about half an hour of walking up and down the airport trying to figure out where to get a taxi, I finally took the plunge and walked outside the airport. At that moment I felt very vulnerable, as if walking out of the airport meant that there was no going back, only going forward. And I guess the expression on my face told everyone around me that I was American, at a loss, and couldn't speak French. HELP! A guy waved me over and found a cab for me. Thank God, I had run into people who felt sorry for me. It was a portent of things to come. I would look for people who felt sorry for me the entire time I was traveling. I figured people who pitied me would be more helpful.

When I got into the taxi, I didn't know how to say, "Can you please take me to my hotel?" All I did was pull out a piece of paper where I had written the name of the hotel. The driver seemed to know where we were going, and we were off. It was a very long and very, very quiet taxi ride to the hotel. The sign on the hotel matched the one I had written down, and I paid the cab driver with some francs I'd exchanged from dollars at the airport, kept my receipt, and walked into the lobby.

I didn't see anyone I knew.

For a moment, I thought I might be in the wrong hotel, but then I went to the front desk and signed in. No problem, my reservation was there, so I was in the right place. I went to my room and dumped my stuff before heading back down to the lobby, where I sat down and waited to see who would show up. Finally I started seeing some of the crew. Then I saw Greg, another producer, and Bert, and I started to get the information I was waiting for.

Many of the crew were sick. They were staying at another hotel. Apparently some of the food they'd eaten in Africa hadn't been cooked enough. The whole thing sounded like a Three Stooges episode. The crew was finding it hard to keep up with the contestants; the contestants were doing anything and everything they could to get ahead. And sometimes they were doing things that hadn't been anticipated. Problems arose that could've been normal production issues, but they were complicated by the fact that it was a race. There was no stopping it now, no matter how screwed up it seemed to be. So the pressure was on us to fix things as we went along. I had a briefing with Greg, and I found out that Alison had also been called to join the race and help out as needed, so I would be seeing her the next day, which made me very happy. Then I went off to see the crew at the other hotel.

The crew didn't look good at all. One of my favorite sound guys seemed particularly ill. But I have to say the people that seemed to fare the best as far as I could tell were the South African crews. The four guys whom I'd worked with remotely for three years on *Wild Things* were used to hanging out with wild animals in Africa, and they seemed to take everything in stride. I remember Michael, a South African cameraman who always had a cigarette in his mouth and a smile when I came by. "Hi Debz!" he would say to me. The nickname stuck. I liked it.

Poor guys, everyone was sick. It was really sad. They crew looked tired and beaten. When I went to the hotel, some of the guys were just sitting on the floor looking really green. The crew was happy to see me, especially since I had brought some Cippro, an antibiotic I'd picked up for myself to have on the road. I put on my "nurse's cap" and let them know everything was going to be fine as I passed out the Cippro. Many of them knew that I would do anything to make the situation better. And they were very grateful for the antibiotics. I figured I wouldn't eat anything that looked suspect on the road, so I hopefully wouldn't need the pills.

After I visited the crew, I went back to the hotel, where I saw some of the contestants. One team looked very upset, and when they saw me, they wanted to talk to me. They came to my room and told me they were eager to quit the show. I was stunned and didn't quite know how to react, particularly since I had only just arrived. They told me that they were not getting along—they just didn't like each other—and they didn't want to move forward. Sadly, I wasn't listening to much of it; in my head a little voice was shouting that I needed to get a film crew in my room to film what they were saying. This is good stuff; this is what we needed. At the same time I expressed concern and sympathy for the couple. I told them to hold on a second and left them in my room. I ran out of there looking for a crew, and I happened upon Greg and a field producer. I explained to them that there was a team in my room that wanted to quit, and we needed to get it on film. They immediately went to get a crew that wasn't sick. I headed back to my room and realized that I'd left the couple in there with a lot of confidential information about the show. For all I know they could've been rifling through my stuff. What a bonehead move! But nobody else thought of it, so I kept it as my little secret. When I got back, it didn't look like they had gone through my stuff, so that was good. The writer, video crew, and producer came in and talked to the contestants in the little ante room of my suite while I shut the door to my bedroom and waited for them to leave. At least they could have some privacy. I'm sure they argued in front of the cameras, but they were ultimately convinced to stay. When I opened my door, they were just leaving, and everything seemed fine.

There was to be a production meeting to talk about the next phase of the shoot, that is, what we were doing in France. We found a small café that squeezed in the entire crew and staff (about thirty of us in all). I can't imagine being the owner of a place in France that's overtaken by Americans so that they can have a meeting. During the meeting, I found out what the producers wanted my role to be. They wanted me to check in with the contestants, count their cash, time their arrival, and generally see to their needs. In fact, the meeting was just getting everyone together to talk through what was going to happen on the race, reviewing any changes and challenges that would be coming up. It was the only meeting I remember participating in. After that, there was little time for a complete team meeting. Some of the guys were still feeling a little sick, but like all the cameramen I've ever known, they powered through their pain to keep the show going.

But first things first…

I had to hit an ATM machine or a bancomat or whatever they call them overseas.

I needed cash. Since I had left too quickly to get a cash advance or per diem, I needed some paper money to take with me because I would be paying for myself (meals, taxis, phone, incidentals, etc.) along the way. I took a walk from my hotel to an ATM machine. It was all in French, but somehow it made sense to me, and I was able to get some francs out of it. I checked in with Los Angeles and told them that everything was fine and that I had arrived safely. I filled them in on the contestants wanting to quit and how that had ended up working out.

One Year of Reality and How It Nearly Killed Me

After another night, we were continuing the race again in France. As we drove to location, I realized that I hadn't paid much attention to where I was. I was in Paris—one of the most romantic cities of the world, replete with beautiful scenery and amazing restaurants—and all I was thinking about was the day's shooting. We ended up on a boat on a river, and I was hanging around in the background, trying to stay out of the way while the crew set up the shots for the contestants. Finally the contestants arrived.

They seemed to be as happy to see me as I was to see them. I counted their money and did what I had to do, and then tried to walk away. But the contestants followed me and wanted to talk to me to see what was going on. I was the only one on the trip with whom they had any established relationship. I was what I like to call "Friendly Fire"—they felt like they could talk to me and tell me anything. And since I'm a bit of a chatter box, I was happy to talk to them too. This started annoying Bert and the producers a bit. I had to leave the area so that they could continue filming because I was a too much of a distraction. I went outside and hung out with one of the new soundmen I had met on the show, a really nice guy. "Do you know where you are?" he said.

"Sure, France."

"Uh, yeah, but do you know where this is?"

"No," I said.

He told me that we were behind the Notre Dame, and then he pointed it out to me. I had to get a picture. I went to the University of Southern California, whose arch rival in football is Notre Dame. Okay, it was Notre Dame in South Bend, Indiana, but still... So I put my USC cap on, and he took a picture for me. Good times.

I only remember eating once, during the production meeting at that café. I was always running around. I don't know if I had that much to do or if I was just plain running around looking important. I've always hated standing around aimlessly, so whenever I didn't have something to do, I took on a new task.

One of those tasks was collecting the trash.

This was a new show and everything had to be kept confidential, including all the clues the contestants were getting. Anytime they had an envelope or a piece of paper with anything about the show or the show logo on it, and they wanted to throw it away, they gave it to me. Nothing could be thrown into the trash that could possibly clue some reporter in on the details of the show. I had never heard of this on any other show before, but it made sense not to leave any clues about the show lying around in case someone in that country ended up finding them and perhaps publishing the information on a website or blog. The race was going to air on television after it was over, so it was important for nothing to be given away. That's why anything even peripherally related to the show needed to be accounted for. I didn't know who was traveling except for on CBS Executive, so we erred on the side of caution.

I also started to collect the shot videotapes. I would either send them home or make sure that someone from the production had them shipped. We had "fixers" in each country that assisted our field producers and put the shoots together. So there were times when I relied on the fixers to take care of shipping the tapes back home, along with the occasional bag of *Amazing Race* trash. At least we could get rid of the trash in Los Angeles. As the contestants continued the race in Paris, I had another job to do.

I sent one of the crews home.

I took a detour from being with the crew and the race to escort one of the teams to the airport. We had lost a couple of contestant teams already, so we didn't need as many camera crews. In fact we had set things up early on so that our crew would be depleted as the contestants were eliminated. We just didn't know beforehand which crew members we'd be sending home. We figured it would be based on the teams that were eliminated. But it didn't end up working that way.

There was a camera crew for each team, and they did a bit of switching around, depending on what the producers wanted or the strength of the camera team filming the contestants. Well, it turned out that every time a team was eliminated from the race, this one particular camera crew was the last one to be with the losing team. They were sort of seen as bad karma for the contestants, and no team wanted to work with them. Somehow the contestants had a say in who was eliminated, and I sent this crew back. For the crew guys, it was like getting fired. Why them? It was hard to explain that the contestants considered them bad luck, but it was true. They had some outstanding costs that they paid out of pocket. I went to the ATM at the airport and got some money out to reimburse them. They didn't live in Los Angeles, and I felt it would be easier to buy back their receipts than for them to carry them home. It wasn't much, just a hundred francs or so.

One Year of Reality and How It Nearly Killed Me

After I left the crew to board the plane, I had to catch up with the production.

I can't remember the details of every moment I was on the trip, but the facilitators had organized vans and cell phones for crews and staff. The cell phones came in handy because we could stay in touch while on the move. I was usually stowed away in the last van…at the last moment…as late as possible. Sometimes this was good. It gave me extra time to strategize and think about what was going on. However, at one point we made a large move to a castle in France that required a train trip. The host and I were left behind. I got the feeling that we had been forgotten. We kind of looked at each other, and I made an executive decision to get us on a train to the next location. I left a message with one of the facilitators about what I was doing. So I purchased a couple of tickets for us, and the host and I had a long ride to our next location. We didn't do much bonding, but we both got some sleep. I can't remember the name of the location, but I do remember finally stopping at the train station and getting off the train. It was like something out of a foreign film. Here we are in the middle of the road, tracks on either side, with a lot of luggage (the host had to have wardrobe options) and no one in sight. I knew that someone was supposed to pick us up, but wasn't sure where. And in truth, it was the first time I had ever been on a train, so I had no idea where to go next. We looked around, leaving our luggage within eye shot, and then we started to slowly struggle forward, carrying a couple of bags at a time. We did this for a few minutes until we finally met up with our driver.

It felt good to be in the van, but I was really hungry at this point. It had been a day, and I hadn't eaten more than one meal since arriving in the country. The host was hungry as well, and we did a quick stop at a store to get some food on our way to the location. We were behind, and I didn't want to hold up the host, so I just grabbed some chips. I really needed to get to the bathroom, but I knew there wasn't time for it. Once we got to the castle, the host was dropped off, and I went in search of a bathroom. I went into the bathroom in the tourist area, but it was just a private room with a floor and a drain, not your standard bathroom—no toilet seat, no nothing! I wasn't sure how to go. I wasn't potty trained with just a drain. So, not knowing the most elegant way to go to the bathroom, I took off all of my clothes from the waist down, including my shoes, and set them aside so I could squat over the drain. I did my business and was thankful that I lived in the modern world with plumbing. I would've never survived in the olden days. I returned to the location where the race was being run. I hadn't seen much of the contestants that day and wanted to make sure I stayed in the background. Once the shooting was finished, and the race had ended for the day, the crews packed up and went to the hotels. They were tired and hungry.

The only restaurant at the castle/hotel where we were staying was closed to the crew.

I couldn't believe it. The crew was kind of cranky at that point. They would have been cranky regardless, but they were extra cranky that they weren't able to eat at the fancy restaurant at the hotel. People who were staying at the castle for their vacation wanted an elegant night of fine dining, and the thought was that the crew would destroy that. I begged the maître d' to let them eat. I put on the big tears, sad look—what I call the poo-poo face—and it seemed to work. He told me that the chef was not pleased, but he would stay around to help feed my crew. No one had made reservations for them, and it was very inconvenient for the restaurant to stay open, as they only had so much food prepared based on their reservations, but they did it.

Crisis averted. Kind of.

So my crew, who were like the Beverly Hillbillies, overran the restaurant. We were not dressed to the nines; in fact, we were kind of grimy. We did the best we could, but the crew didn't have much in the way of wardrobe, and it was a hot and dusty day. So we certainly upset the other guests who were already dining. Alison, who had joined us in Paris, was working with the crew and talking to them about what they'd be doing the following day, walking all around the restaurant to make sure that everyone was eating. We became loud. The maître d' asked me to tell my people to quiet down and act civilized since we were disturbing the others. I told him I would do my best. I pulled Alison aside and told her of the maître d's request, which was ignored. The best thing I could do was walk away. I didn't have any dinner. I was trying to figure out how to communicate with everyone about the call times for the next day, since the crew was spread across three hotels.

We had a mini production meeting with the producers, myself, and Alison. How could we make sure that everyone knew when they had to call in?

I suggested call sheets, but that idea was quickly rejected. There was no time and no easy way of putting them together and distributing them. The crew would be asleep by the time we had them ready. We figured out a way for them to automatically calculate their call times. The contestants knew that once they stopped, it would be twelve hours before they started again. The rule of the show was that from the time the team crossed the line, it would be exactly twelve hours before they started the race again. So we worked backwards and told the crew their call time would be ten hours after their contestants arrived. Alison and I worked through the night and got just a couple of hours of sleep. We would be up the next morning with the first crews to head off to the starting point.

It was 3:00 a.m. I was feeling kind of shaky, but that quickly changed when we had to start waking up the crew. Some of them were already prepping, some were not. We didn't know all of their room numbers, so we had to jump behind the registration desk and go through the register to see who was where. Then we walked around the grounds to wake up those who were still asleep and get them going. We also distributed videotapes for the day, along with any paperwork they needed, and got them in the right vans to go to location. We did this for the better part of the night, trying not to wake the other patrons at the castle. We pretty much overran the joint, and in a last ditch apology, I left a $350 tip at the registration desk, thanking them for putting up with us. I made sure to call Terry in the States when I had a chance, letting him know what had happened at the castle in case there were any issues. And by the time the sun was rising, the crews were off and running, right along with the contestants.

Next stop…Tunisia.

Okay, I'll admit that I wasn't quite sure where that was. I knew it was in Africa, but not where. It was the only location I hadn't looked at on the map. I had a small map of the world with me, and I was able to find it. I hadn't packed any scarves or anything, so I was worried about what I would do to show respect for the local culture. I did have a lot of black, though, so I figured I could at least wear that while I was there. But first, I had to help the crews get out of France.

I met all the crews at the airport along with the contestants, who were trying to get the tickets they need. In addition to the crews that were following the contestants, we had a second unit crew. This was the crew that caught everything that might have been missed by the other ones. Sort of the "overview" crew that got a chance to see everything that was happening rather than focusing on one team. This crew had extra gear, including a jib camera (a camera on a small crane that could get those sweeping location shots), which was pretty big, and other extra gear. This was one of my first biggest challenges: getting the crews and all their gear on the plane for the next country. The second unit crew had so much gear that they had to pay for excess baggage. They didn't have the money for it, and there wasn't a producer to come up with the funds, so it became my job to negotiate and pay the fees. I actually tried to avoid negotiating the excess baggage fees since I was such a green traveler. I know the guys probably had a better idea than I did about how to get good rates for all the extra gear. I also felt the additional pressure of having Bert hovering over me.

Bert wasn't in a particularly good mood; after all, the race was not really going as planned, even though it *was* going. And I was sure that he was under constant pressure from the network that I cannot even imagine, so I didn't want to add to his angst or mine. Once he got his tickets and moved on, I went back to work. After the crew had all boarded the plane, I bought tickets for Alison and me and got on the plane for Tunisia.

Over the course of my three days in France, I'd eaten all of one meal and one bag of chips because I was running around trying to fix things. I wasn't sure I was going to make it.

I started to fall apart.

CHAPTER 5
COMPLETELY LOST

All countries are different. The people are different, their views are different, and their food is different. So it's no wonder that each country has its own "scent." This was true when I arrived in Tunisia. My first impression was that the air was heavy and sweaty and smelled of hot dirt. Of course, it's a country in the desert, so that made sense. And the heat was heavy. Not humid, but thick, yet surprisingly comfortable for how hot it was. This seemed odd since I was wearing all black. I had on black shoes, black leggings, and a large black sweatshirt with Mickey Mouse on the front. I felt it was the best outfit to wear while I was there.

Most of the crew was already at the hotel, so I was lagging behind. I reached my room and really wanted something to eat, but there wasn't time. I met up with Alison at our hotel. I had a few minutes to take a quick shower, and then I met up with her in my room. We were still playing catch up on the production. Trying to make things run more smoothly, with better communication, ensuring that we didn't have any catastrophic problems.

I liked her energy, as mine was already lagging a bit. I would stay up late at night and check in with the office in Los Angeles and fax them info whenever possible. I also tried to keep up with my mounting receipts and expenses, which were stacking up. And then I would have to work with our Los Angeles-based travel agent and get information on all the possible options the contestants could choose when they started traveling. I needed to at least know what options were out there, so it was important for me to get up-to-the-minute information. It was late; I was hungry and tired, and knew I had a lot to do.

Then Alison said something I could not believe: "I could really production manage this whole show."

She told me this as I was sitting down and organizing myself. I stopped for a moment thinking,

What? Production manage the whole show? There are already two production managers on this show. I wasn't sure what she really meant, but she seemed to be saying she could do a better job than what was being done up to this point. I wanted to raise my hand and say, "Hello, this is the production manager in the room with you. If you want my job, you shouldn't be saying that to my face." I wasn't happy at that point. I know that Bert had wanted her to come on board, but I didn't need someone overtaking my world, plus I thought she was light years better than I was based on what I could see of her work. I was jealous. I started to get paranoid, thinking that I was on the brink of being sent home. But I didn't say anything. I had one edge over her. She had never worked with Bert before. I had, and no matter how much he might prefer her, he relied on me. At the moment, though, he "favored" her and didn't pay much attention to me. I was grateful to be under the radar somewhat, but I felt as though my efforts were going unnoticed. Even though there was this unspoken animosity between me and Bert, I still wanted kudos here and there.

Alison and I talked about the next day's shooting, where the crew was going to be, where we would be, and what we would be doing. We were going to be at the Coliseum in El Jem, and then we'd have a down day to catch up and rest. I would be there to check in on the contestants at the end of the race.

It was early morning, and I was with the crew who was setting up for the end of this part of the race. The second unit was setting up the jib and lights and whatnot in the Coliseum (one of the most well-preserved Roman Coliseums, quite stunning). It was a big affair, much like a feature film setup with lots of lights, trucks, and people running around to set up the shots. The field producer responsible for Tunisia was one who I had worked with on *Wild Things*. He spoke French, which helped with the foreign crew, as they only spoke French Arabic. I arrived on set and was recruited to help with the transportation, the parking of vehicles, and assessing the crews' needs. Then I was put into a van and asked to check out all the hotels—there were three—and to make sure that all the crew had rooms and there would be no problems.

The first hotel was for the crew and was relatively close to the Coliseum. The person at the registration desk did not understand a word I was saying, but he let me look at the reservation list. The crew was checked in, and everything was fine. Of course, I couldn't read anything on the list or understand what the man was saying to me, but I kept repeating the names and number of rooms, and somehow I got through the information and felt comfortable that there wouldn't be any problems for the crew. I thought I would take a peek at the rooms and ran into a couple of camera guys who shared one of the rooms. They had just done their laundry and they had strung a rope across the room to hang their "undies" to dry. I asked them how they cleaned their clothes. They said that since they had to carry their clothes it was easier to just take a shower with them on and scrub them down clean and hang them up to dry each night. I was just throwing clothes away and couldn't imagine showering fully dressed. I had a lot of respect for them. They were tired, hungry and a few other things, but had a great attitude. I just loved the overall attitude of the crew. I said my goodbyes, then I headed over to the place where the contestants were going to be staying, and everything was fine there as well. That hotel was even closer to the Coliseum, about a mile or less. Even though both hotels were so close to the location where we'd be shooting, vans still needed to be assigned to pick up the crew and contestants and bring them there.

The third hotel, where the producers and I would be staying, was thirty kilometers or so away from location. Since I wasn't familiar with translating kilometers into miles, I figured it was really far.

It was a very silent, long drive since the driver and I didn't speak the same language. Just a lot of smiling and an occasional pointed finger to something interesting by the side of the road. A couple of times we had to slow down and stop for what looked like military people. The driver would hand them some paperwork and then move on. I figured that once I checked out the last hotel, I could set up my computer and get to work. It was a grand, spacious hotel, and it looked like something out of a lavish 1940s movie. Very cool place. I checked into the hotel and the driver left. I went to my room to set up and got a call.

"You have to come back to the Coliseum right away," Greg told me frantically. "You have to check in the contestants." It had taken the better part of the day to look at the hotels, and now I had to rush back to the Coliseum. I raced down to the lobby of the hotel to get my driver, but he had already left. I went to the front desk and said, "Taxi?" The person behind the desk pointed over to a man, and together we went out to his car. I could only give him instructions in English, "I need to go to El Jem, the Coliseum at El Jem."

"El Jem, okay," he said. And we were off. We drove for about ten minutes, and then he pulled over.

I just sat there.

I wasn't quite sure what to do. Obviously he hadn't understood me, and now I was in the middle of nowhere with no idea what to say or do. Then he said something to me that I could not understand. I was in a hurry, and was feeling a great deal of pressure to make it back to location in time. I started to cry a little. "El Jem, El Jem, El Jem." I just kept saying it over and over again. Finally the guy got out of the car, opened the door, grabbed me out of the car, and literally pulled me across the street toward a building. I was a little concerned about where we were heading and why, but I couldn't think of a better option. Inside the building was an open area where a lot of cars were jammed together and parked in a disorganized fashion. He took me into the middle of this mass of cars and people, all of whom were yelling at me, wanting my business. He led me over to another guy and talked to him for about five minutes. I envisioned what he was saying. "She's American, take advantage of her. She wants to go to El Jem, but you can probably get her for a few hundred dinars, after all, she overpaid me by a whole lot." I don't remember how much I gave him, but I know it was way too much. I had a tendency to overpay, as I could never understand what they were saying the price was. So I'm sure I screwed myself on that one.

Next thing I know, I'm in the new taxi driver's car, and we're on our way somewhere. I figured that anywhere was better than where I was, even though I didn't understand what was going on. I was just praying that I was going to make it to El Jem. I'm a little slow, but it finally occurred to me that the name El Jem reminded me of something I'd heard in the past... I couldn't figure out why. I was completely stressed, but my mind did not race with worries about getting killed or robbed or left in the middle of the desert. I was more concerned about making my destination on time than whether or not I was in mortal danger. I also wished that I was a whole lot savvier at traveling than I was turning out to be. Finally, after what seemed like an eternity, I saw the road signs for El Jem and knew I was going to be okay. The driver stopped at the Coliseum and started talking.

But I had no idea what he was saying.

I figured he wanted to get paid. I was fumbling for my money and trying to figure out how many dinars I needed, when someone from El Jem came up to the taxi and started to translate for me. "Fifteen dinars. It's fifteen dinars, madam." I was so grateful. I gave the driver twenty and thanked him, then got out and paid the translator another five and thanked him as well. "That is my restaurant over there," he said. "You come and visit."

"Okay. I cannot come now, but maybe tomorrow." I knew I probably wouldn't—after all, I was staying at a hotel that was thirty kilometers away. But I was sincere in my insincerity. Nevertheless, I ran off to the location. I was there in time to see the crew running through what would happen for the finale of this portion of the race. The host and the producers were there too, and everyone was waiting for the contestants and the crews that were following them. The field producer was getting up-to-the-minute information from the drivers and people who were watching the teams so they could be ready.

As the contestants neared the finish line, tension was running high. I'm sure I missed something that had happened at rehearsal since I was out and about, but Bert was especially nervous. At one point, he took the steadicam operator's camera and started to film the proceedings himself. Since he had been a cameraman in the past, this was the moment for him to get the shots he wanted. The cameraman hung out in the background with me. We just looked at each other and shrugged our shoulders. We also had torches going for effect. It looked pretty cool. We were all crowded around the finish line, and one of the torches that was lit was knocked over, starting a small fire in the Coliseum. We put it out right away, but it was a scary moment.

One by one the contestants crossed the finish line. I don't think anyone was eliminated at that point, but the time they arrived would be the time they got to leave the next morning, twelve hours later.

I started going about my business of checking in with the contestants regarding their money situation and receipts. Each time I started this procedure, I was always pulled away for some reason or another. Eventually I stopped even worrying about their money. If it was so important, no one would try and tear me away from it. It might've been a psychological play on the part of the producers to make the contestants think that if they cheated by using more money than they were given, they could be eliminated.

After all of the contestants had arrived, the crew didn't leave. They hung around and interviewed the contestants, asking them how they were feeling, what happened, and what they thought of the other contestants. So it was going on sunset when the crews finally started back to their hotel. I went with a couple of producers back to our hotel. It had been a very long day, and it was great to be able to relax on the drive back to the hotel, since I would need to start the second part of my day as soon as I got there.

Within moments of my arrival, Greg came over to me and said, "You need to stay with the contestants. We don't have anyone staying with the contestants."

"Why me?" I asked. "Who else can we send?"

Well, I could think of a few people. I just felt that I was a bad choice because of all the work I was doing to figure out where they are going next. I didn't want them to come into my room and see confidential information. I certainly did not want to repeat what had happened in my room in France, even though the contestants hadn't gone through anything then. I felt like a teenager who's been asked to sit at the kiddies' table for Thanksgiving. I wanted to hang out with the producers and get caught up on plans for the next couple of days, but instead I had to watch the children. I understood why they were sending me; I just felt a little sorry for myself.

Dejected, I checked out of my hotel and got into a van with the field producer for the Tunisia shoot, Jared. I think he was going to check on the contestants to make sure the hotel was okay and meet up with the facilitators to ensure the next day's shoot would go off without a hitch. He was pretty cool. I got into the front passenger seat and Jared was behind me in the back seat, near the sliding door. The producers and executives were all hanging around outside the hotel, talking about where to go eat dinner and have some fun. Man was I feeling sorry for myself. I wanted to cry.

And then I really did.

Just as I reached back for my seat belt, Jared shut the sliding door of the van. The door slammed into my fingers…all of my fingers. I was so paralyzed with pain to the point that I couldn't talk. I was trying to say, "Open the door," but it wasn't coming out very loudly, and I started crying. The third time I said, "Open the door," Jared heard me and realized what had happened. He opened the door. Bert had seen everything, and he ran over to see if I was okay. I was fine, sort of. I kept my hand above my head so that the blood would drain away. I couldn't tell if my fingers were broken, I just knew I was in terrible pain. We drove away. I didn't think of going to a hospital, let alone know where we could find one. And no, no one offered to rush me to the emergency room because I insisted I was okay, even though I could barely talk and the pain was crazy awful. I NEVER wanted to be a problem. As we drove away, it was quiet for a moment, with the exception of my sobbing, and then I heard a little crying in the back. I knew it was Jared.

It was obvious how bad he felt, and through the pain and tears I told him that it was okay, that I knew he hadn't done it on purpose, that I'd be fine. But I think we were both crying for reasons other than my fingers. We were tired, him especially, since I felt that his part of the show was the hardest, with the lack of English-speaking people. And from what I could tell, he was all over the place trying to keep things together. We were both tired, frustrated, and the job was overwhelming. So much to do, so much to fix, and no time to do anything except keep the race going. I call it putting Band-Aids on bleeders. When something goes terribly wrong, you solve small problems, but the big ones still persist.

So we would patch up problems as they cropped up and redefine rules as the show crept along. I knew everything would get solved after the race was over; in the meantime, I just had to do what I could.

I arrived back at the contestants' hotel. By that time the excruciating pain in my fingers had gone down to a painful throbbing, something I could handle. I'm double jointed, so I maneuvered my fingers around to check if anything was broken. I could move all my fingers and joints. I breathed a sigh of relief. It was dark and the hotel looked like a haunted mansion. I checked in with a guy who did not smile or speak. I tried to crack a couple of dumb American jokes that went unnoticed. He just gave me a key and pointed me toward my room.

I passed a television room that had some local programming, and then I walked out into a courtyard. There were ten Tunisian men sitting around staring at me. I stared back. When I got to my room, I heard that they would be serving dinner shortly. So I raced into the dining room with the contestants and ordered two lamb dinners. I had only eaten one good meal on the trip, and I wanted to make up for lost time. For the first time in days I realized I was starving.

It was actually a good thing that I hung out with the contestants. It was the first time that I was able to get to know them a little better without any cameras around. No one seemed to hate each other at this point, or at least we were all eating together in the same area without any open conflict. And it was good to hear them talk about their lives, what they were doing. I realized that they were opening up to me more than they would to another field producer, probably because I'd known them from the beginning, and because I didn't have a camera trained on them. I put in a call to one of the producers and said that he should be here at the dinner filming because there was a lot of good conversation going on that could be an asset to the show. A cameraman and producer finally showed up to film the contestants. And all the while, I was just eating everything in sight, making up for all that fasting.

Later, after everyone went to their rooms and I was in mine, I realized that I couldn't get on the internet or fax anything. The phone lines were routed through the front desk, and all I could do was make calls. It almost felt like a day off, and then one of the producers came in and confirmed that we were going to have a day off the next day, and I needed to hang with the contestants. I was fine with that. I didn't feel the pressure of whatever was going on with the producers who were trying to figure out the race. I had high hopes that the next day would be restful.

I didn't know what to do with the contestants, but I had to keep them occupied somehow. We all got up kind of late and puttered around, and then I took the group of them for "walkies." You know, what you do with your dog when you take him or her for a walk. The major difference was that the contestants weren't leashed. They didn't need to be; they were pretty well-behaved, following me around. There wasn't much to do in El Jem to fill a whole day, but I knew where we needed to go first.

We needed to visit my new friend, the translator.

We had lunch at the restaurant owned by the guy who helped me with the taxi cab driver. He remembered me and was excited to see me. We were a pretty large group, and I noticed that some of the cameramen were having lunch there as well. So it was cool to see the crew and contestants eating together. And the owner was so nice and generous to us. He even gave me a gift of a sand rock. It was beautiful, and I appreciated it. I was happy to have kept the promise I'd made to him the previous day. I didn't really eat, though—I was too busy watching the contestants, making sure they didn't go astray. I didn't have any rules to go by except to spend time with them. The second unit crew was working that day, and we saw them driving around the Coliseum, taking footage of the sights around town. I took a picture with the host and the contestants as a memento.

After lunch we started walking around and did a little shopping. El Jem was definitely tourist savvy. And of course, my interest was in the men. I can't imagine why a basketball scout hadn't checked out Tunisia before, because everyone was so tall. There was this one shop owner who kept following me around and showing me jewelry. He knew very little English, but one phrase he knew very well: "Marry me." So while we were shopping, this guy would shout out, "Marry me!" every now and again. I'm not sure if he knew what he was saying, but you could say that it was my second proposal of marriage. The first one came from a drunken cameraman who was so enamored with my talent of burp talking that he'd asked me to be his wife. Forget that he was already married. If I wasn't in a foreign country and the shopkeeper guy spoke more English…who knows. He did quiet down a bit when I bought a couple of things from him.

One of my favorite memories of *Wild Things* was when the field producers came back from traveling to exotic locales with little gifts for the staff. Jared gave me a carved elephant that to this day, sits proudly on my dresser. So I knew I had to follow in that tradition. I had to bring home some things for the staff members who hadn't been able to come with us.

Once we were done shopping, we did some more walking away from the square. I just started to walk around the Coliseum, thinking there might be some other shops or something set up. There were a couple of stands with drinks and ice cream, but that was about it. And then I saw it in the parking lot.

A camel.

He was standing there with his owner, and there was a sign that said something like, "One dinar for a ride on the camel." It wasn't a big parking lot, but I figured it would kill a lot of time. I got the contestants to join me, and asked if they'd be interested in riding the camel. I wanted to do it myself, but the animal took a particular dislike to me—he tried to follow me around and kept making evil snorts at me. So I passed. But a few of the contestants had some fun while the rest watched. That killed about thirty minutes. The ride was basically once around the parking lot. It reminded me of children taking rides on ponies in zoos. The worst thing was the camel was really smelly, not pleasant at all.

After the stint with the camel, we walked back to the square and to our hotel. On the way back, I noticed that some of the contestants were starting to look unhappy. I could tell that one of the contestants in particular seemed down, and was hanging back from the rest of the group. I wasn't sure what to do, so I tried to wait for him. But he refused to be engaged in conversation, and I finally let him alone. I could tell he didn't want to be there, and eventually was eliminated with his partner. A lot of school children were looking at us as we went, since we must have made for a strange sight. We waved and smiled and made it back to the hotel. Those men were still hanging out there. That was creeping me out more than anything. Didn't they have jobs? What are they, some type of Tunisian mafia? Do they have to hang around here all the time? They would stop talking and just sit there and stare, like zombies, as I went to my room. It was pretty creepy.

I was starting to get stressed out again.

I received a phone call from one of the producers a little later. "Did you give the contestants camel rides?" he asked.

"Well, yes. There was a camel in the parking lot, and we were killing time."

"Well that was something we were going to do tomorrow, and it was supposed to be a surprise." He wasn't very happy. I defended myself. "Well, I didn't know that; I'm not with you guys, so I'm not up to date with what's being planned."

Still, I felt awful about making such a screw up. Later that night, I met with a couple of the producers in my room. They told me they needed me to check in the first teams really early in the morning. I would be picked up at the hotel at 2:30 a.m., taken to the Coliseum, and then a van would take me to the next location. One of the producers got a call while he was with me and had to head straight to the next location for the following day. He was at my hotel, not his, which was really far away. He didn't have a change of clothes with him, so I gave him a shirt and jacket, assuring him that they were men's clothes. He took them and thanked me. I didn't see him again until we reached the next country.

I was feeling stressed and bummed that I had to be up so early, which meant I wouldn't get any sleep because I had to call into the office that night and come up with the usual travel options. I walked out into the courtyard to see the staring men and a few of the contestants hanging out. I sat down with a couple of them, who asked me how I was doing.

I made the mistake of answering them.

"I'll be fine once we're in Italy." It was an off-the-cuff, conversational remark that instantly sent cold spikes up and down my spine. I could tell that I was turning red, and I felt my eyes fill up with tears. "Oh my God, I can't believe I just said that. Please don't say anything, please don't say anything," I begged them. "I could lose my job." They promised they wouldn't, and they acted like they didn't know what I was talking about. I didn't want to repeat myself. All I said was, "Never mind," and went back to my room. I told one of the producers what had happened, and he said, "It happens, you're not the only one." So I felt better. I hadn't given away the show; they just knew I was stressing, and they felt bad for me.

I was so bothered by my comment, which made me really wish that I didn't have to hang around the contestants, but it was my job and I needed to focus on doing it well.

That's what mistakes do. They wake you up to your faults, and you either resolve to do better or you crumble under the pressure. Somehow I did both. I felt a little crumbling, but wanted to do a good job. Again, the fear of the show going into the toilet because of something I had done was real for me, and I edged a little closer to it.

I packed myself up and checked out of the hotel at 2:30 a.m. Again, the guys were hanging out and staring. Now it didn't sit well with me. But I was dressed in the same outfit that I had worn for the last couple of days. I walked out of the hotel to get picked up by the van. And I waited for a while.

No van.

I decided to walk to the location. I didn't have time to figure out where the van was or why it hadn't arrived. My cell phone was dead anyway, since I had been using it to talk to the office. So I couldn't reach anyone. Since the contestants and I had walked over to the Coliseum the previous day, it wouldn't take long to get there, right? It was under a mile.

But it was very dark. There weren't street lights like we have street lights, and the road was made of cobblestones or something really bumpy and uneven. And I didn't want to walk near any alleyways in case there were some not-so-nice guys who were hanging out, waiting for someone like me to show up. So I walked down the middle of the street. If there was going to be a car, I would at least see it and get out of the way, but I wouldn't make it easy for someone to whisk me into a room or be kidnapped. I was really feeling scared. But I just kept pushing forward. It was very quiet, save for my rolling suitcase maneuvering over all the bumps in the road.

And then I noticed that there were people following me. It was the first time I had really felt that I had made a mistake. I should have waited for the van or figured something else out; I should *not* have gone on by myself. I really thought that since I was being followed, it was a matter of time before someone would overtake and attack me. I remembered seeing a guy in a brown "friar" outfit. I couldn't see his face, but he got up from the sidewalk and started following me. My heart was pounding in my throat, and since it was hard to see, I couldn't tell how close I was to the Coliseum, where the race would start up again. I felt that the "friar" guy would probably be okay—after all, he was probably a good guy if he was a friar. But I still walked as fast as I could. The cobblestones were uneven, I didn't want to fall, and dragging my luggage as well as carrying my computer and the trash from the show was getting to be burdensome.

Then I finally saw the Coliseum, and I knew I was safe. There were a few people milling about. The art director, Greg, and a few worker bees were setting up shop. Just as I arrived at the Coliseum, I finally tripped and fell. I twisted my ankle and hurt my knee, but I was more embarrassed than in pain. After that, I limped around to see if anyone needed me to do anything. There was nothing for me to do. I was a little mad that I had been told to get up so early if there was no need for it. I found out later that "friar" guy was one of the security guys who'd picked up on the fact that I was walking alone. So in a weird way my instincts had been correct.

Well, soon the contestants were off, the crews with them, and I was on my way to the next hotel. It was a long drive through the desert and I would see an occasional sign. And then I saw a sign for "Tatooine" and couldn't believe it. It finally hit me where I had heard the town El Jem and now Tatooine. It was from Star Wars. I wasn't sure which came first, the name of the town or the movie. It made me smile to think about it. I did not have the benefit of a working cell phone because it was dead, so the only way that anyone could get a hold of me would be through the hotel phone. During the ride I learned that the contestants were off to an oasis, where they would spend the night camping. And some press would be at that location; the network had invited them as a way to promote the show. I wondered if they'd been asked to sign confidentiality agreements too. The crew would be going to the hotel at the end of shooting, and then the next stop was Italy.

One Year of Reality and How It Nearly Killed Me

I had been out of touch with the producers while I was babysitting with the contestants, so I wasn't sure what was happening, where I was supposed to be, or what I was supposed to do. But since I had ended up at the hotel, I figured I would set up my little office, make sure that the crew had rooms, and wait for a call or some information. I was the only person from the American crew hanging out at the hotel. It was a beautiful place with a swimming pool. I wished I had some time to enjoy the moment and go for a swim. I decided to take at least some advantage of the downtime and go to the café to get some food. When I entered the café, I saw many members of the Tunisian crew, including a couple of guys who I figured were in charge. Jared was off on the shoot, and couldn't translate for me, so for a while, all I heard was French Arabic, which I couldn't understand at all. But I still hung out with the staff, trying to get an idea of what they were saying. They were laughing and having a good time. By then, I was sitting at their table and eating with them. I still didn't understand a word they were saying, but I smiled when they smiled and chuckled when they laughed. And then their conversation changed, something was happening. It appeared to be a big deal because it was getting dark. Now, even though I didn't speak their language, I could tell something was wrong. A couple of guys were on their cell phones but they didn't appear to be panicked, but their voices were very serious.

As I ate with the crew, a girl came up and sat with us. It turned out that she was the daughter of the Tunisian facilitator who was with us, and she was studying at a Los Angeles College. She just happened to be home while we were filming. It was great to finally meet someone who spoke English; the crew was nice to me, but they just didn't know how to talk to me. I asked her to fill me in on what was going on. She told me that one of the contestant teams were lost, meaning that they hadn't returned to the finish line in a timely fashion. So Bert had hopped into a car and was driving around to try and find the contestants. That seemed pretty bad given the fact the press was there and I'm sure Bert wanted to find them so it looked good to the press. I had to keep believing that we would all make it to Italy okay the next day.

Everything turned out fine. The contestants finally arrived at the location, and Bert made it to the hotel, although he was very upset about what had happened. But the team was found, Bert was found and we could move on.

It was morning and the crews and contestants were moving forward. I was waiting for the producers and the second unit crews to arrive and get them on the plane. There was a flurry of activity. There was a lot of equipment and luggage and people to manage. Thank goodness I didn't have to do that. All I had to do was try to get better deals on excess baggage and arrange tickets for the crew members who didn't have them. Our travel agent couldn't get every ticket done in advance, and often I would arrange to pick up the tickets myself and pass them out to the crew, which is what I did this time.

The crew was always sleep deprived, but they still seemed pretty cheery. Tired, but doing their thing. I had a deep respect for that. There were a couple of second unit crew members whom I had grown to appreciate, and I looked forward to seeing them. The sound guy always had a great joke to tell me, which was a highlight to my day. But my nerves would always do flips when Bert would walk into my world in the airport. I was always nervous that he was watching me, wanting to criticize or intervene for me. I would wait until he got his ticket and took care of himself before I took care of the crew. When all of the crew members had their tickets and were heading to the gate, it was time for me to get my own ticket. (I had to buy all my tickets along the way since I didn't know when or where I'd be going.) But this flight happened to be full. Again, I gave some big teary eyes and waited while the ticket person helped others. I made a real nuisance of myself. I could tell because the ticket guy kept staring at me and nodding his head. I begged for a ticket and finally he let me have one, and I raced through customs and got onto the plane.

We were on our way to Italy.

CHAPTER 6
FINALLY! HOME!

The plane to Italy did not have a first class section. And this was very disconcerting to Bert, who hated for anyone to be around him, particularly us minions. I can say this with confidence as I have organized and booked many flights for him, and I know what he wants and if he ever got the wrong seat assignment (whether I had control over that or not), it was a bad day with one angry producer. And I knew how he felt about his place in the world. It wasn't that he didn't respect his crew or appreciate them—he just felt he deserved to be in a better class. And he's not alone, all producers and executives are the same. I've had bosses who were quite frankly a pain in the $%@ when it came to airline reservations. It could take anywhere from a couple of days to a week to make one reservation, as they'd nitpick over which airline to take, when, what seat they wanted, and more.

No matter what I booked, it was never right.

Flying to Rome was no exception, even though I hadn't booked Bert's ticket on this particular trip. My stomach was in knots the whole time because I knew that he was upset since I was sitting behind him. I could sense it the entire flight. So I was grateful that we finally landed and he could focus on the race in Italy and not who was sitting where on the plane. And I was glad to be in Rome. It was really hot, a dry heat that really made me sweat, along with everyone else around me.

Of course, the moment I let my guard down and began to take a moment to relax, I felt my hand start to throb again, and I realized I didn't feel so great. My adrenaline had finally subsided enough for me to begin to sense pain in my body. When I got to the hotel, I had to go to work right away. But I was feeling really sick and dizzy, so I called the hotel doctor first. I had never heard of a hotel doctor until I called the hotel and told them I was getting sick. Within the hour, the doctor was by my side, and he checked me out and gave me a prescription for nausea medication. I don't know what his diagnosis was, but I was glad to get some kind of relief. I did have to venture out to the Pharmacia and pick up the prescription, but that was no problem, and it is much easier than it would have been here in the States. I didn't tell anyone about my illness, figuring it was probably from all the stress, and the lack of sleep and food.

When I returned to the hotel, I had to get back to the visas. I did not have a visa for the next country, India, and more importantly, there had been a paper screw up and the South African crew needed visas too, as did two other crew members who had been added on at the last minute including Alison. So I had arranged to go to the Indian Embassy in Rome to get the visas. I had very little expectation of even getting mine, since it had taken us a full six weeks to get visas for the other crew members. I was going to try to get the rest of us into the country as visitors; that way, it would hopefully take less time. Now remember, this was before 9/11, so it was a lot easier to try and push the envelope. I don't think I would attempt most of the things I did overseas after 9/11, but at this point I had nothing to fear except the wrath of Bert and an entire network. In my deluded, workaholic haze, I had decided it would be better to get arrested and thrown into an international prison than to endure a very ugly dressing down and firing for stalling the race.

I didn't have a driver take me around, nor did I have any support from the Italian production company, since everyone was assigned to the shoot. I had to do this alone and taxi wherever I needed to go. I was draining my money pretty fast. I had to get more cash so I hit the hotel and the ATMs to get the money to pay for the visas and any other incentives that might be needed. I also had to get my own visa expedited, so I came up with a plan. It was sophomoric, but I couldn't think of anything better to do.

I decided to tap into my short-lived college acting career, and play the part of the completely helpless female who is very, very desperate for help. Hard to do for a 6' 2, 240-pound woman over forty who looks like she can play on a football team. But I still felt that tears could always evoke a little male sympathy. That probably puts women's liberation back a few decades, but I consider it a useful gadget in my little toolbox of life.

I planned on having a nervous breakdown, with the hopes that my river of tears would wash me and my poor friends into India. I only had a couple of days to accomplish this. Whatever was happening on the race took a back seat to getting the visas. It should have been easy to get the South African crew's visas since their information had already been forwarded to the embassy from Washington D.C., and it should have been as easy as getting the passports stamped. The scary thing was that I had to hold onto the crew's passports so I could get them stamped. I figured that would only take one trip, and hopefully only a couple of extra trips would be needed to get the visas for me and the new crew. At some point, I had notified my Washington contact that three extra visas were needed, so hopefully that would help as well.

But I had grossly miscalculated the whole scenario.

The embassy in Rome had no paperwork for the South African crew, let alone for the rest of us. They had never heard from the embassy in the U.S. Panic set in. I was able to make an appointment to see an embassy official. This is where my "acting" would come in handy, I hoped. But I ended up bypassing the acting and went straight to reality. I told this gentleman that I was trying to help my friend's crew get visas, that Washington was supposed to send the information to make this happen, and that the rest of us were coming in on visitor's visas. He asked me why I would help my friend, and I told him I just wanted to help the crew, and I would be so grateful if he could help me. I didn't want him to think I was part of the crew because I was hoping to get a visitor's visa as opposed to any other type of visa, which would be more difficult. I said all of this with a lot more words and a lot more tears, to the point where I literally melted in this man's office. I was hysterical. I told him that I'd been working with India for several years, and I needed to make a miracle happen. I started to turn red from crying and was doing that thing where you are trying to get air, but you can't because you're sobbing too loudly. The gentlemen, in his official, dignified attire, sat down next to me and tried to console me. He told me to come back the next day and that they would do the best they could. I could tell he really wanted me out of his office. I think I just about made *him* cry.

I went straight back to my hotel and started making calls, sending faxes, and doing whatever I could do. I called Washington D.C., I called San Francisco, I called our India contacts, I called our South African contacts, and I sent e-mails pleading with the Indian Embassy in D.C. for help. I even had the crew fill out extra forms and get additional passport photos. The one thing I tried not to do, which was very hard, was to pass on the panic I was feeling. I am considered to be stoic and rather stone-faced most of the time. I usually don't pass on my anxiety. But this time it took everything I had to say "No problem, we're going to get this done." Even Bert didn't feel like it was going to happen, but I don't recall anyone putting together a plan B in case it didn't. It just had to happen; there was no way out. We all needed our visas... Usually that sentence ended in an "or else," but this time it didn't. We all needed our visas.

After having sent out numerous faxes and paperwork, with assurances that information from Washington had gone to Rome and that all would be well, I went to the Indian Embassy again and turned in the paperwork. They still had not received anything from Washington. I called Washington again, just catching someone, who re-sent the information to Rome and sent a copy to me in case there were any remaining issues. I went back to the embassy and handed in the new information. They had the fax too, and they said it would take a few days to process. Again, pushing my panic button, I told them that it needed to be expedited, recounting the tale of what had happened the day before at the embassy. They would do everything they could, but I needed to pay for my visa and the ones for the two new crew members. So I was off to a nearby ATM to get some cash. I walked around for about twenty minutes before I finally found an ATM and got the money. Once I paid the embassy official, I was told to come back the next day. I called Washington again and begged them to stay in contact with Rome to get everything finalized.

Meanwhile, the race was still going on. I had completely dropped out of the loop. While everyone else was running around Rome, I was deeply ensconced in the whole drama involving the visas.

I returned the next day, and still nothing had been approved. I had no idea what else I could do to move things along at that stage. I had cried, paid through the nose, and tried to play the charmer... What next? Well, there was an extra fee that would help expedite the process (why didn't they tell me that before?). So once again, I found myself looking for an ATM. I could never find the same one twice. Rome is so beautiful and ornate that I kept getting lost left and right, and it was hard for me to find any points of reference. I would turn one corner, then another, and everything would start to look the same. But I was always able to find my way back to the embassy and give them money and get a receipt. This time, they said they would "for sure" be ready when I came back the next day. So I walked away from the embassy breathing a sigh of relief. Finally, everything would be settled.

But there was a glitch.

I didn't know *when* they'd be ready, and the race would be going from Rome to Milan the next day, and from there to India. So the crew had to have their passports before boarding the plane to India. I hated having to carry the passports around for so long. I didn't want to lose them, and now I would have to catch up to them in Milan. Time was running out.

I decided that I would get to the embassy as soon as it opened and be a nuisance until I got the passports. Again, the possibility of being arrested and jailed in an international prison seemed preferable to having to tell the producer that the race had to stop because I hadn't completed a simple (yet complicated) task. But since I couldn't do anything about the visas that night, I decided to actually venture out for dinner and maybe catch up with a couple of people I knew, which is exactly what I did. I found a nice little restaurant nearby where some of the crew members were eating. I hadn't seen them very much, especially in a social setting, and I felt a little weird about inviting myself to sit with them. Who knew if they really wanted me to? But I was craving some company and relaxation, so I joined their little party. After all, this could be my last meal with the crew. If things didn't go well, I might get fired, arrested, or something else I hadn't calculated on. After a couple of hours it was time to go back to the hotel and get ready for the next day.

By the time the crews had checked out of the hotel and were off filming the race, I had just packed myself up, checked out, and grabbed a cab to the embassy. I figured that it would be good to have everything with me so I could go directly from the embassy to the airport and get on the first plane to Milan. I was only carrying a small suitcase, a satchel filled with *Amazing Race* garbage, and a laptop computer, so I was compact, but it clearly looked like I was ready to leave town. I arrived at the embassy an hour early and sat on the steps waiting. A policeman who passed by (or, rather, a man in a blue uniform) didn't like the fact that I was sitting there, and he told me to leave. So I walked around the embassy area for about an hour. I didn't want to go too far because I didn't want to get lost. I basically went around the block a few times, and I finally had the chance to notice the beautiful architecture and the statues that adorned one particular corner of what I called embassy row. I'm not sure what they were, but I want to say there were statues of the furies on each corner. I would have to look at a picture and do a little research on that one. My mythology is very rusty. And whatever mythology I knew was probably from *Xena: Warrior Princess.*

In any event, the embassy finally opened, and I was first in line. The passports would be ready in a bit, but I needed to pay another additional fee. At this point, I can't even remember the reason for it—I just paid it. I was lucky to have some cash left over. The person at the counter said it would be a couple of hours, and that I should come back at 11:00 a.m. Because there was no place to stand around, I left and walked around some more, planning to return at the aforementioned time. I didn't have a watch, so I went down the street to a jeweler and bought one. I couldn't believe I didn't already have one given how critical time was on this show. I guess I relied pretty heavily on hotel wake up calls. But I wanted to be back at the right time to get the passports, so that I could meet the crew members as soon as possible.

I returned at 11:00 a.m. and there was another glitch.

They needed even more money. For what, I'll never know. At this point, I feel pretty comfortable saying it was professional bribing. They knew I was desperate and would pay. They would release the visas to me as soon as I made the final payment. I was out of money at this point and needed to go to another ATM. So I took my suitcase, satchel, and computer and went off in search of the ATM. I walked around the block and finally found one. It took a while because the first two I found didn't work. When I finally found a functional one, I also discovered that I had hit the limit on my ATM card and could not access more money. I had to use a credit card, which I had never before used to get cash from at an ATM. I couldn't remember the code. I wanted to go into the bank, but I thought it would look suspicious since I was carrying way too much stuff. Banks are very well protected, and I didn't want to cause a disturbance. I decided to call the production office, which would be calmer now that the crew was gone, to see if they could help me out with cash.

Then I hit a huge problem.

Every time I arrived in a new country, I was given a cell phone and a list of everyone else's phone numbers so that we could all stay in touch. The same had been true when I hit Rome. But I could not find it. I must've left it at the hotel or lost it in a cab. I needed to get money, get on a plane, meet the crew, hand out their passports, and get on the plane to India without any missteps. I was starting to shake from nerves.

I took out one of my credit cards and just started trying random pin numbers. I don't know which numbers I hit, but I finally chose the right ones and was able to get the money from my card. I was sweating by then, and I nearly cried out in relief. I was going to get the money, race back to the embassy, and get the visas. Crisis averted.

And then I realized I was lost.

The embassies didn't look the same. I was in the wrong place. No matter where I turned, it looked like the same street I had been on, but the flags were all different. I felt like Jimmy Stewart in *Vertigo*. I was running around trying to find the flag for the Indian Embassy. I must've looked panicked, sick, or something, because I caught the attention of a police officer (blue uniform), who started to speak to me in Italian. I had no idea what he was saying, but I just kept repeating "Embassy, Indian Embassy." Then another officer (grey uniform) came over and started talking to the first officer. I tried to walk away, figuring they were just having a conversation. But the blue officer said something that sounded like "Freeze," and my heart stopped.

Maybe this was the arrest I had been envisioning.

They took my suitcase. I had in it some of the passports that had been handed to me. They went through them and my underwear and everything else right there in the street. I just kept saying "Embassy, India. Embassy, India. Please, I need to leave." I think I looked pathetic enough that the grey uniformed officer said something to the blue uniformed officer, and they sort of let me go. They gave me directions, and somehow I understood them. One block up and turn right. "Great. Thank you!"

I walked to the embassy as fast as I could. I was waiting in line to make the final payment for the visas when I caught sight of the Italian coordinator for the show. Apparently, the taxi driver had returned the cell phone to the production company (the cell phone had a label with their name on it) and the driver had told him where he'd dropped me off. We chatted for a moment, and he told me that the producers were absolutely panicking about the visas. I told them I was getting them, and would be leaving soon. He wanted to give me the cell phone, but I told him that I was going to be in Milan in a couple of hours, and that I'd meet the crew at the airport. I wanted him to pass the message on to the producers because I didn't want a tongue lashing from Bert to make me lose my focus. I just needed to get this task done. Finally, I paid the final bribe—I'm sorry, payment—got the passports, and headed to the airport.

When I arrived in Milan, I didn't know where to meet the crew, but I knew which airline they were taking to India, so I bolted for the waiting area. Finally, I ran into them, and they were very relieved to see me. I think bets had been made on whether or not I'd make it. Relieved, I gave everyone their passports, and we were off to India. I cannot express to you how it felt when the tension left my body. It was like I went limp, empty, hollow, nothing there. My muscles couldn't move and my brain was dead. I was so happy the race could continue. I had dodged a major bullet. We were all able to connect to our next flights.

Being on the plane to our next destination with nothing to do was the only relief I had until we arrived in India.

I was so looking forward to going to India. For three years on *Wild Things* I had worked with two of the facilitators via phone from India. I enjoyed speaking to them and had always hoped to meet them one day. So the prospect of finally meeting them in person was exciting. But my good mood quickly expired when we arrived at the airport and the India staff gathered our passports. For a moment I panicked. Why are they taking them from us? Then I remembered that of course they were supposed to take them—this is where we would get the visas for China. We still did not have permission to go to China. There hadn't been enough time to process the visas before the crew left the States, so the China producer had told us that we could get them while we were in India, since we had some time to take care of it. So of course they needed our passports. In the U.S., I had sent all of the applications and copies of everyone's passports to India, so that they could start the process while we were on the road. It should have been easy to just have the passports stamped, as the applications should have been signed off on before our arrival.

But it didn't happen that way.

No one had taken our information over to the Chinese Embassy to start the process. The person responsible for the visas insisted that he hadn't been able to do anything until he had the actual documents. The panic button hit me again, but this time it was ten times stronger than it had been in Rome. This was an issue for the entire crew, not just a few of us. I was really angry. How could this have fallen through the cracks? I was angry that it hadn't already been done, and even more so that the person responsible was making excuses. He didn't even try, didn't ask. We'd been assured that everything was taken care of, but it wasn't. This was huge.

So after getting situated at the hotel, I planned on heading straight for the Chinese Embassy. Lately I had been spending more time in embassies than I had with the contestants or crew!

India was nothing like what it looks like in travel brochures. It was very unassuming. But what struck me the most was the amount of people who wanted my attention and money. Everywhere taxi drivers were trying to wave me down and get me into their cabs, and once I got into a cab, people were lining up in the middle of the road to try and shove things into my window so that I'd buy them. And people off on the side of the road were also selling things and vying for my attention. In Los Angeles, there might be one or two people hanging out at the end of an off ramp or by a fast food joint asking for money, as well as the occasional person selling flowers and balloons in the middle of the street, but in India, you could multiply that by a thousand. And at the sides of the streets were people living in tents or whatever shelter they could manage. I even saw a man going to the bathroom by the side of the road. I'm assuming it was near his tent. The poverty was intense. But the women were always dressed beautifully, no matter how poor, in vibrantly colored fabrics.

So I was grateful to get settled into my hotel. I was not looking forward to going to the Chinese Embassy, but I wanted to make sure that we got our visas. I didn't trust anyone but myself at this point. And since I was now responsible for making it happen, I wasn't just going to sit around waiting for our Indian contact to handle the visas. I knew that he wouldn't push the envelope to get things done. He didn't have the same kind of panic I had. I couldn't make him see that the world would end if we did not get those visas on time. We had some time to get them, but we were also hitting a weekend, which worried me.

The trip to the embassy was totally different from the trip to the hotel. It was beautiful. The embassies here were large and beautifully landscaped. I even saw monkeys running across the streets. It took some time to find the Chinese Embassy, but when we got there, I noticed that it was completely enclosed by a high, protected fence. I wasn't sure how we were going to get inside.

Then I saw it.

Think of Lucy's psychiatric office in the *Peanuts* comic strip. That was what the visa office was like for the Chinese Embassy. It was outside the fence of this beautiful embassy, and it was like a shack with two people helping the long, undulating line of people who were standing outside. No chairs, all sun and heat. We waited for a while, and I walked around and noticed where the servants' quarters were located and checked out the people who were milling about outside of the grounds.

We were finally able to get in line and—after a long wait—hand in all of the passports and paperwork. It was quite a stack. Obviously they weren't ready for something like this. In fact, they hadn't heard about us at all. That seemed strange since I understood that our Chinese producer and facilitator had been in touch from China to make sure this was going to happen according to plan. It was Thursday, and we were told that they would have to communicate back to China to get the approvals, which should take a day, and then we should be able to get our visas on Monday.

Should, should, should. I hated that damn word. It wasn't consoling, it came with no guarantees, and it left plenty of room for mistakes, laziness, and ineptitude. It's a crappy word. And yet I've often used it myself as a way of avoiding a commitment. I determined then and there never to do so again.

And it wasn't something I wanted to tell Bert either. We SHOULD be able to get the visas by Monday. *SHOULD!?!?!?!?!?* was pretty much his guaranteed reaction. It wasn't a "should," but a "must". If we didn't get our visas on Monday, we would have to stop the race. And since no embassies or officials worked on the weekend, Friday was my only chance to make sure anything got done. I had pulled off a miracle in Rome. Could I do it here, in India?

I contacted the producer for the China shoot, and told her that I was panicking and wasn't at all sure this was going to happen. She was one of the few producers I didn't know. I had worked with most of the others on *Wild Things*. But I wasn't sure how she would deal with the news that her plan of getting the visas in India was kind of falling apart. To my amazement and respect, she handled it well. She told me that we had done everything we could; there was nothing more we could do. She would get in touch with her contact and make sure everything was in place on her end for us to get the visas on Monday, but only so much could be done. While she was upset, she was rational, and I appreciated that. If she was panicking, she didn't verbalize it quite like I did. However, Bert was less rational.

Since I was completely obsessed with my own drama of getting the crew visas for China, I wasn't aware of how the race was progressing. I had been either hanging out in my hotel room or at the embassy. It was a nail-biting waiting game. Alison was pretty much handling all of the logistics for the contestants, which I think I was supposed to be doing before the entire visa mess came up. That is, she was checking in the contestants at each location and being an ear for Bert. She updated me on what was happening with them. The crew and contestants were going to leave New Delhi for the Taj Mahal, and then return to New Delhi before moving on to Thailand. She went on with the crew and contestants while I stayed at the hotel and caught up on paperwork and came up with different travel scenarios for how the contestants could get to Thailand and around India.

At right about that time, I had an ugly run in with Alison.

As I've said, I thought she was very capable and had a lot of respect for her talent. However, like a few other people on the shoot, she had never worked with Bert before. She wanted to do everything he asked of her. Well, as much as Bert and I had trouble getting along, I was able to help settle him down while still keeping him informed. I believe there is always a good way to deliver bad news to an angry producer. And even if I wanted to "murder" my boss at times, I wanted to do everything I could to make him look good and make *me* look good. So Alison and I were alike in that way. It's just that she didn't know how to handle his yelling or his orders. It was starting to wear on her.

One night I was in my hotel room, and was talking to Laura in the States on my cell phone. I needed to talk to someone not in the hurricane of the show and to tell me everything was going to be okay. I also had a production cell phone, and was on hold with our travel agent in the States, who was coming up with information on potential travel scenarios for the contestants. Then Alison called me on my room phone.

She was clearly upset, so I set both cell phones down on my bed and took the call. Alison was crying and yelling at the top of her lungs, telling me that Bert needed the airline information NOW! and couldn't wait any longer for me to get it. I told her that as soon as I had it I would call, just as I always did. But she just kept on crelling (a cross between crying and yelling) about how bad I was making her look. I just kept on repeating myself. I was getting pretty pissed off, because they should have known by then that I always gave them everything as soon as possible. But I also had it in the back of my head that Bert was probably paranoid about me after what had happened in Rome. We finally hung up.

Even my friend had been able to hear Alison screaming at me from the phone that was resting on the bed, so you can imagine just how loud and upset she was. I told my friend I had to call her back. The travel agent was getting the info faxed over to me, so I hung up with him too. I called the production office in the States and spoke to Phillip.

"She's been Berterized," I told him. "Oh no." he replied. He knew exactly what I meant. It was that one time when you got reamed up and down for nothing. And since Bert never went one on one with me (I'm sure this was because I matched him in height and weight), he always took it out on someone else. She was doing her job, and doing it well. He should've called me if he had a problem, but instead he'd picked on someone from whom he could get a reaction. I felt bad for her, but I knew that she'd be on to him in a couple of months or so, just like everyone else.

It was great to have the weekend to catch up on things. I spoke to Terry, who told me that we were going to need to lose another crew. I knew that, and had already picked one out. It was random. They were the only two crew members who were not getting visas to China. They would end in Thailand, and then head home. I even spent a little time trying to get my ever-expanding pile of receipts together and sent back some *Amazing Race* trash. Everything seemed to be on track for getting the visas on Monday. I had not heard anything except that the information had been sent to the embassy in India and all they needed to do was process it. I even had time to go out with Alison and do a small bit of shopping and get some fries from McDonalds. I was happy about that because I felt bad about how she had been treated and our disagreeable phone argument.

While I was out, I tried to take pictures of some sacred cows that were milling about the hotel, but they kept running away from me and a cameraman that I had met outside. It was like we were chasing them around the property.

I took advantage of my five-star hotel room and took a relaxing and very long bath. It almost felt like a day off. But with every few moments of good came something bad.

I had another problem that sent me into a panic.

I could not pay my hotel bill. The front desk told me that my credit card was maxed out, and I needed to find another way to pay. I gave him all my credit cards and none would work. I called the India facilitator for help, but they said they were tapped out of money. Even our travel agent wasn't able to assist me, though I can't remember why. I called Terry at the office and told him that I needed a cash advance so that I could move on. He said, "No problem." He asked me to check in with him on Monday to see what they could do. Monday was turning out to be a very busy day.

But the weekend wasn't over yet. The race was still happening, and I had to meet up with the crews at the airport in order to facilitate excess baggage fees and check on the contestants. I always had to show my ticket out of India in order to enter the airport.

After a while, the guy started to recognize me and just let me through. The entrance to the airport always had a long line, and everyone would just stand there, enduring the heat. Since I had no luggage, I just bypassed everyone in line, channeling my inner pushy American. It was the longest weekend I'd ever experienced in my life. It felt like I'd never get out of India.

At least Monday started out well.

I was able to see the Academy Awards. It was crazy to watch them live in the morning, but so cool. I got room service and watched the show while I got ready to go to the embassy. I stopped by the facilitators' home first to say hello and see their setup. It was the one thing I was determined to do since we still hadn't met in person.

Unfortunately, my day was downhill from there. The embassy had not processed the visas for China. The crew needed to leave on Tuesday for their next destination, but there was nothing that could be done. I called the producer in China to let her know and started the phone chain so that everyone would find out that I didn't have the visas. It would take another day to get them, but there was a hitch. The visa office was only open on Monday, Wednesday, and

Friday. So the earliest we could get them would be Wednesday.

NO WAY! Not acceptable. I was screaming that in my head while trying to have a pleasantly firm conversation with the visa person. "Isn't there some way we can get them on Tuesday? Everything is riding on this. I'll do whatever is necessary to pick them up tomorrow. You don't have to open the visa office, and we won't tell anyone, just please, please, we need the visas on Tuesday."

After much pleading, begging, and crying, he said, "Yes," and told me to meet him there in the morning, and everything would be fine.

Would, would, would. I like that word. Very firm and committed.

But there was nothing I could do about Monday. I could not get the visas that day no matter how hard I tried. The permission had not come through from China, and neither the visa person nor the Chinese producer could get a hold of anyone in China to get the approval. So I had the good fortune of going to the airport to see the crew off to another location in India while I delivered the unhappy news to Bert. We had our first ever showdown. He was furious. He got up in my face, telling me, "What am I supposed to tell the network? Why did you screw up [my words, his were more colorful] like this? I can't believe it." He was mad as hell. I stood my ground, staring at him, and said, "We did all we could, I could not do anything more."

He threw a few more choice words my way, telling me that everything was my fault. I was incompetent, he said, and I was ruining everything. I just stood there silently, trying not to have a breakdown. It wasn't my fault; just my turn. A decision had been made prior to the beginning of the race that didn't end up panning out. The blame game wouldn't change that. I felt like this was sort of his moment to unload all the gripes he'd had about me over the years. So I became his punching bag for a moment. It was painful, but I got through it. I did decide in that highly emotional moment that I wouldn't be doing a second season of the show. Still, I knew that I needed to hang on and finish this one.

We must have been quite a sight, and I noticed quite a few people watching our exchange. For one thing, we were easily the two tallest people in the airport. You couldn't miss us. And as the argument started, people began to back up, as if anticipating that a fist fight might break out. It was rather surreal to get a "dress down" in front of a lot of strangers over something I could not control. The crew, who also observed this uncomfortable moment, got on the plane and left.

I went back to the hotel and had a good cry alone. I needed to organize the travel plans for the crew that we were sending home. Of course, when I broke the news to them they wanted to know why they'd been chosen. I had to assure them it was not because they were bad or incompetent, it was just that someone needed to go and they'd been selected. Bert was furious that we were losing them, because he wanted all of the crew members he could get. I wasn't sure if Terry had spoken to him about it. I felt very much in the middle, but it was too late to do anything. Terry had told me what to do, and we couldn't go back. It was one more reason for Bert to hate me. At this point, I'm sure he wanted me gone or at least strangled.

In the meantime, my credit cards were at critical mass.

I called my friend, Kelly, who had been paying my bills for me, and I had arranged for her to go the production office to pick up some sort of cash advance check so that she could pay off some of my credit cards. I called her while she was at the production office filling out an expense report. AN EXPENSE REPORT!!!! I told her that I was the only one who could fill out an expense report because I was the only one who had the receipts as backup and the credit card bills wouldn't have nearly enough on them to show that I needed more money since the billing cycle closed at the middle of the month. I had spent so much more than what would be reported. I wanted a CASH ADVANCE. I was furious that the accountant had asked her to do that. I told her to go home and forget about it, and that I was going to deal with the production company myself. I called all of my credit card companies (thank God there are international numbers on the backs of the cards). I explained my situation, and one of the companies raised my limit so that I could at least pay my hotel bill and check out when needed. I had no idea what my credit limits were, I never spent a lot of money on the cards, and generally paid them off in full on time, so I didn't care about hitting a limit, but I had reached the limits on all of them, which scared me. Even though I knew I would get reimbursed, you never know how much you'll end up getting back. There are producers out there who have reputations for not paying people back, even for legitimate expenses.

I called Terry, furious, and told him that I was coming home. I was broke and had no expectation of getting money soon enough to pay for another hotel, so I was getting on a plane, which our travel agent could presumably cover, and coming home. I could not continue the race in this fashion. He agreed. And besides, China was the last country for which the crew needed visas. Once they had those, they wouldn't need me anymore on the road.

Tuesday swung round, and I was more than ready to get the crews' passports. But when I got to the visa shack with my Indian counterpart, no one was there. Now I was officially panicking. However, when we were there on Monday, I had scoped out the area. There was a way to get onto embassy property through what looked to be the servants' quarters. And while there was a fence that separated the quarters from the actual embassy, there seemed to be a dip in the fence that I could use to climb over into the embassy courtyard. I called Bert to let him know that I was on top of everything…literally. I told him, "I'm at the servant's quarters, and I'm going to jump the fence and knock on the door and see what happens." As I hung up I heard him saying, "Don't do it! Don't jump over the fence." I guess he figured it was just as crazy as I did. But the race needed to go on.

Luckily, as I approached the fence, our visa person finally made it to the visa office. Everything had been approved. It was just going to take a bit of time to get the visas onto the passports, but we would have them. I was incredibly relieved. I went back to the hotel to call some of the crew to let them know that I'd soon have their passports. They could either come see me later in the day or get the passports at the airport when they went on to Thailand. Because of the whole visa situation, Monday had to be a day off. The crew members were so happy to have the day off that they all thanked me. Now I hadn't given them anything, it was purely a matter of circumstance, but I appreciated the sentiment. The crews were working long hours, and it took a lot out of them to carry all that equipment as well as their own belongings. A day off wouldn't kill the race.

Some crew members were traveling ahead of the contestant crews and that night I had to meet them at the airport to help them with excess baggage payments. This time, I had no ability to get out money with credit cards, just my ATM card. Alison and I hooked up and went to an ATM on the way to the airport. Now you think of ATMs as something you can easily get to since there are so many and you can access one off the street or in a 7/11 or Walgreens. In India, we went into a bulletproof ATM outside of a McDonalds with a guard standing watch. It didn't exactly instill confidence. Well, the dollar was pretty strong in India, and the maximum amount I could take out was $300 U.S. dollars. It took me five times to put in my card and withdraw money to get the $300. It was a lot of bills and I didn't have a purse big enough to hold it, so I stuffed the money into my bra, since no one would look there if I was robbed. Alison took out money as well, since she hadn't tapped all her resources yet. (I can't imagine how much she must have spent on the road.) So we had the cash and helped the crews get on the plane. It was funny to be able to whip money out of my bra and hand it to the airline person. I also realized that it was the best place for carrying all my important documents. Ever since, I have always carried my passport and money in my bra. I'm big enough to keep the money from moving around, and if my purse was stolen, at least I'd have identification and some cash.

I met most of the crews at the airport the next morning and gave them their passports. And once again, they needed help checking in to the New Delhi hotel, getting settled, and getting fed. The contestants were haggard and tired, but they greeted me with smiles. Soon, all the crews and the producers would be on the plane to Thailand, and I would be on a plane back to the States. I couldn't wait. And I didn't say anything to Bert about the fact that I was leaving. I figured Terry would tell him, or he'd figure it out on his own. I was too tired for that discussion.

Bert was one of the first ones on the plane. I had to help the rest of the crew pay for their flights since credit cards were not always an acceptable form of payment. I passed out the last of my cash from the previous night and got more from my ATM card to make sure I had enough. Finally, I had everyone on the plane except for two people. They were part of the second unit crew. They were finishing up the rest of the India shots that had been requested by the producer, but they were running late. I could not get a hold of them by phone, but we heard from the driver that they were on their way. Well, the plane was getting ready to take off, and I knew they needed to be on it, because I had no idea which plane they'd be on next. The other hitch was that once a plane was loaded, the ticket counter changed to another airline. It was driving me crazy. So I kept the ticket person engaged. I started to do a "stupid American" comedy routine to try to keep them laughing. No one else was boarding, and there were only two seats left in first class. So I went about purchasing the tickets for the guys, taking my time while paying for them, doing anything I could to delay the plane from taking off.

Finally the last two crew members showed up, and I gave them their tickets and paid for their excess baggage. They whipped through customs and got onto the plane in the nick of time. It took a moment for me to absorb the fact that everyone was gone except for me, and that I would soon be home.

A few minutes later, someone came out of customs.

There was this old man slowly walking out, coming my way. I didn't know him, and yet he was clearly gunning for me. I froze, wondering what had happened in customs that needed to be fixed. In the ten or fifteen seconds it took this guy to reach me, I had already run at least ten scenarios in my head as to what was about to happen. Someone was sick, equipment was broken, a contestant was ill, the plane was being delayed, and Bert was wondering where I was… But the guy simply handed me a note, without smiling or otherwise acknowledging me, and then walked away. I kept the note for about two years because it's the one thing that could always set me off into roaring laughter. It read something like this:

"Bert is upset that you have people in first class. Try not to let that happen again."

It was signed by a field producer. It made me laugh, it made me mad, it made me say, "That's it! ENOUGH!"

I went back to the hotel. I knew I had a few hours before they would land and get situated. I called Terry in the States and told him about the note and why I'd bought first class seats for those crew members. I "killed it" to get everyone on the plane and told him everything that had happened. I did all this work, and all I got was a lousy note. "If you have to fire me," I said. "I'll understand." Of course he wasn't going to fire me. But I did tell him that I planned on yelling at Bert as soon as he called me. I knew him like I know the back of my hand, and I had no doubt that I would be getting that call. Which, of course, I did. And Bert didn't get five words out before I went on the defensive. "I've worked for you for three years, and you don't think I know the rule about first class?" I asked him. "Don't you think I'd do whatever it took to make things work and keep them going? Don't you think that I would have put them in coach if I had a choice? Don't you know by now that I do everything I can to make sure you're happy, and that I'm not trying to irritate you? Well, don't you?" That was pretty much my rant and my chance to unload a bit after all the years of hard work I had put in for him.

We didn't speak again until right before I left the show. I heard from people on location that he was asking them if I was all right, if I was having any problems. I guess the fact that I had finally chosen to stand up to him had made an impact. Good. I sent the producers travel information on the contestants and told them that I was coming home and wouldn't be able to give them any information until I was back in the States. I'm not sure that anyone knew I was leaving. I had told Alison, but I didn't think to tell anyone else in terms of the producers. So I don't know if they were shocked or not, but there was nothing I could do. I was broke.

I caught a break.

I left the next day. I found out I could get into business class, so I did. The trip had a couple of legs, but I didn't care, I just wanted to get home. When I hit the second leg, the longest part of the trip, I was tired and cranky, but at least I was in business class. And I love having the window seat. I get nauseous on flights, so having something to lean on, like the side of the plane, always made me feel better. Even though

I'm tall, I didn't care about leg room as much as I did having a window and an easily accessible barf bag. I didn't have any Dramamine, and I couldn't find any in the airports I was passing through, so I just had to grin and bear it.

I thought I'd get some rest once I got home. I was wrong.

CHAPTER 7
TRIUMPHANT RETURN – WIMPY ENDING

There are two things that I've heard about what it's like to return to the States after traveling internationally. First, you gain such a great appreciation for the United States and the freedoms we enjoy that you want to kiss the ground. Second, the jet lag is pretty bad.

When I would have crews come back from overseas on *Wild Things*, I tried not to call them for at least a day to give them time to adjust and get some rest before coming into the office and wrapping up their work. Most of the time that didn't happen, and I would have to get the crews to come in and download as soon as their plane landed. But if I could get away with giving them a rest, I would. I was hoping for the same kind of break.

I didn't know what jet lag felt like. I was pretty okay on the flight back to the States. I was tired, and my stomach was a bit off kilter, but I figured it was just because I'd been eating plane food for the last fifteen hours. I was able to relax and sleep through the five movies on the flight.

While I didn't kiss the ground when I returned, I did kiss my pillow. I went to sleep as soon as I got home that Friday afternoon. But I did have to get up the next day, because Kelly had organized a trip to the hair salon for me. I had been feeling pretty dirty, and my hair was definitely showing the wear and tear of the road, particularly since I hadn't taken any hair products with me. I slept up until the time I had to leave for the salon. My stomach was still doing flips, and I had something to eat to calm it down.

I've had many embarrassing moments. My most embarrassing was in sixth grade when I broke the string off my cello at a talent contest and decided to sing a solo with no preparation. It wasn't until I had finished the first verse of "There's No Business Like Show Business" that I realized it was a bad idea.

Now, the second most embarrassing thing in my life was about to happen...

I met my new hairdresser, J.C., who was a friend of Kelly's, and we had the usual beautician conversation about what I'd been doing (without giving away any details of where I had been), what I wanted to do with my hair, and any entertainment gossip we could come up with. When she started to wash my hair, my stomach was really bothering me. I kind of ignored it, figuring that I'd forget about it once I finished getting my hair done. As J.C. started putting color into my hair, a truck hit me. The room started to spin, not all the way around, but fast and short half spins, and I really needed to go to the bathroom. I hit the bathroom, and as soon as I came out, I told J.C. to get the color out of my hair because I needed to go to the hospital. Now, how I knew that is beyond me; it just came out of my mouth. "Do you want me to call 911?" asked J.C.

"No," I said. "Call my friend, Rhonda."

Now Rhonda is one of those friends that you want to have around on momentous occasions. Every woman thinks that they are Lucy and their best friend is Ethel. Well, that's how I think of Rhonda. When my father died, she paid for my airline ticket home.

When she wanted to wish her friend a happy birthday, we stood alongside a hill adjacent to the freeway early one morning and she rolled out a huge, very long HAPPY BIRTHDAY! sign along the hill. Everyone driving on the Hollywood Freeway and around his apartment complex could see it. So it made sense that she was the one I chose to take me to the hospital. I had become the center of attention at a salon I had never been to before, among people I had never met until that day. I went into the back and rested while J.C. called Rhonda, who was in Hollywood. It took about a half hour, but she finally showed up, and I managed to pour myself into her car.

In typical Lucy/Ethel fashion, we drove around haphazardly, looking for an emergency room. Now there was an emergency room only nineteen blocks or so away, but we didn't even consider it. We decided to go to the emergency room I had frequented in the past. It was twenty minutes away, but at least they might have a file on me already. So we went to the ER in Marina Del Rey. I was feeling really awful, something I had never experienced before. It was like having the flu and feeling pregnant all at once. My guts felt like they were in my lungs, and I was achy, dizzy, and incoherent.

We finally got to the emergency room and after waiting what seemed like hours, I finally went into the admitting room to give them my info. Rhonda was with me. I told them that I must've gotten something from overseas, but couldn't say where I'd been, as I had signed a confidentiality agreement. This wasn't my brightest moment in the world. I should've just told them, but I was worried about that stupid agreement.

They took my temperature, and it was 103. I remember the admitting lady saying, "We need to get you a bed!" Well, we went back out into the waiting room, but there weren't any couches there where I could rest. I tried to sit, but my head needed to be on the floor. Instead of lying down in the middle of the waiting room floor, I went out to Rhonda's car and stretched myself across the seats. Since I'm longer than most cars, I left the driver door open and my legs dangled outside of the car.

I don't know how long I was there, but I was told later it was about four hours. Rhonda apparently would come and check on me from time to time, and then go into the waiting room and tell anyone who'd listen that I had been to a foreign country and could be spreading something to everyone right now if they didn't take me inside. Well, finally a couple of guys came to get me with a stretcher. My temperature was high, and something was wrong with my blood (either too many or too few white cells, I can't remember which). They put me on Cippro and gave me some other stuff too. Rhonda was there with me the whole time, and she called my mom. "Hello, Mrs. Wolff?" she said. "This is Rhonda, Deb's friend. Everything's okay, but..." and she proceeded to tell my mom everything that had happened. Rhonda also spoke to Philip, and I remember him saying not to worry about anything, that everything would be okay. I took that to mean that someone would take over for me until I got better. The doctor came in and told me that I had something about ten times worse than Montezuma's Revenge, but that the antibiotics and lots of rest would probably cure it. I had gotten up a few times to go to the bathroom, but I finally became fully conscious at about midnight. The nurse asked me if I wanted to stay overnight, and I told her that I'd prefer to go home. Rhonda helped me get dressed. Oddly enough, one of my shoes was missing. They had put all of my clothes and one shoe underneath the gurney where I'd been laying all day. So we looked around the whole emergency room for the other shoe. Finally I gave up and went barefoot back to Rhonda's car and home to my bed—a bed that I'd hardly slept in since moving to the apartment a couple of months ago.

One Year of Reality and How It Nearly Killed Me

Even though my sickness kept me from going in to the office, I started working again the next day. While lying on the floor of my bathroom (so that I could be close to the toilet), I was on the phone with travel agents and producers about potential travel plans for the contestants. Things were going rather smoothly at last—even for a first year show, *Amazing Race* had been a bit of a mess—but I still had to get to the end of the race, which would be in New York.

I had only been out of the hospital for three days when I got on a plane to New York. I cannot tell you how excruciating that flight was. Since I was nauseous, dizzy, and ill before takeoff, I couldn't imagine what the flight itself would be like. And I absolutely hate going to the bathroom on a plane. So I did whatever I could to keep myself—and my bowels—together so that I wouldn't get sick or need to use the restroom on the plane. Plus, I wasn't eating anything because it would go right through me, and I wasn't about to hang out in the airline bathroom for the entire flight.

A bit green, but grateful, I made it to my hotel room in New York. It was just like the beginning of the race. We had the New York staff prepping, I was on the phone trying to get travel info, staff started arriving and getting ready for the end. We weren't prepping for a wrap party, but the finale, the final run to the finish line for the contestants. It wasn't exactly fun to have people come in and out of my room (since it was the production office), as I ran back and forth from the bathroom to the bedroom, but at least I could do most of my work from bed with the phone and the computer. Finally, after a day or so, I started feeling better and had something to eat. It was a momentous occasion, because when I had to go to the bathroom afterwards, it was actually a good experience. I literally pooped out my entire colon, or at least that was what it felt like. And to be even grosser, it was one long piece that came out that literally circled the bowl. I had never seen that in my life. To top it off, it happened twice. Once I eliminated everything, I started feeling a lot better and could participate in full form. It seemed that the big bad bug had left me.

I also got my out date.

My out date was simply the last day I would be working on the show, which was essentially two weeks after I returned from New York and wrapped up some of the loose ends as best I could. So now I knew when I would need another job. I kept this on the back burner because I had more present problems to deal with.

One of my crews were stuck at immigration in Canada.

One of the race's last stops before New York was Alaska. All the crews and contestants left had made it there, and then they would need to get on planes to New York. There were several different ways to get to New York from Alaska. One of them was Alaska to Canada to New York. It never occurred to me that we would have a problem if a crew came through Canada. The South African crew, which had followed a team of contestants, was stuck in Vancouver, and they weren't being allowed back into the States. Canada was not on the lists of countries for the race, so I hadn't applied for visas for everyone. I still kick myself for not having considered this turn of events, since I had tried to make sure we were covered for any "transition" countries. Canada had never entered my mind. Agh!

But that wasn't even the problem.

I was fortunate to have worked with Canadian Immigration in the past on many other studio shows, so I'd gotten to know the immigration person in Vancouver personally. I gave her a call to see what the scoop was, and what I could do. I tried to explain my situation, and even sent off a quick letter explaining that I had a crew that was transitioning to New York and I needed their equipment to be returned, if nothing else.

But Canada was ultimately not the problem, it was the U.S. Another group of filmmakers had gone through the border a month before and done something incredibly illegal, though no one could tell me what it was, and the U.S. border patrol was leery of foreigners with American equipment returning to the country regardless of whether or not they had visas. Though the Canadian immigration officer I knew was receptive, the U.S. customs people literally refused to take my calls. I tried calling all sorts of customs phone numbers that I had accrued over the years to see if there were any strings I could pull. There weren't. They only thing the crew could do now was get on a plane and go back to Africa with the equipment.

Losing the crew was not so bad in terms of the contestants. The crews couldn't film them on the plane, so they'd just be sitting there. So there would be no loss of footage. But it was still a loss. The South African crew was one of our best, and I knew Bert liked them and that he hated to lose any crews. Plus, they had our gear, and we would have to have it shipped back from Africa. And I would have to let the producers know that we'd lost the crew so that they could compensate for that loss. So I gave one of the producers, who I called "friendly fire," the information about the crew and started researching how the contestants would be returning to New York.

The night before the contestants were going to arrive in New York, I was told that the crews were going to rehearse the end of the show so that they'd have the best camera positions when the contestants came off the train and raced to the finish line. And they were going to do this right before the contestants arrived. So I got information from the airline the night before and passed it along. Early that morning, when the crews were already on their way to rehearse, I received firmer information on which flight the contestants were arriving on and double-checked the times. According to the airline, everything was on time.

But that wasn't true.

As the crews were setting up to rehearse the ending, the contestants had already landed and were on their way... The crews had to literally dive out of sight so that the contestants wouldn't see them and figure out they were in the right place and doing the right thing. No time for rehearsal, plenty of time for panicking. It was a race to the end, not only for the contestants, but for the crew.

The race was finally over.

I stayed in New York for a couple of more days to organize flights for the crews and contestants and settle up any final cash reimbursements that I needed to hand out. While I didn't relax and take time out to "smell the roses," I felt good because I could finally wind down after being amped up for a month. I couldn't wait to get home, finish this job, and move on to whatever was next.

Which didn't take long.

I returned to the production office with the rest of the staff forty pounds lighter and very happy to be back. I had time to actually send out a couple of resumes, and within a week of returning, I had an interview and a job. Not only was it a new job, but it came with better pay, a better title, and more responsibility. But there was a catch. The new job wanted me to start two days prior to my out date. I told Terry about my new job and asked if I could leave a couple of days early. He gave me permission, but I also told him that I would continue to wrap things like credit card bills and the reconciling of travel costs on my off time (read: nights and weekends). Great, no problem.

But there would be trouble, and I sort of knew it.

When we were working on *Wild Things*, anyone who finished their job and went on to another one was persona non grata to Bert. Even though their job had ended, if he wanted them back and they weren't available, he would hold it against them. This was something I had never experienced before. Since production is freelance, you try and get your people whenever you start up a new project, but if someone's already working, you just move on down the list. But Bert held grudges; it was as if he expected his staff to sit around and not work until he called them. It was a weird jealousy thing. When his first production manager quit *Wild Things*, he enforced her contract and made her finish the season regardless of the fact that he didn't like her or want to deal with her. Leaving was never amicable. But my departure seemed to be going off without a hitch. I was waiting for the other shoe to drop, but it never did.

At least not until after I left.

My last day was a Tuesday, and I was cleaning out my desk and organizing papers and folders on my computer, when Bert came into my office. Philip was not in at the time, so it was just the two of us. I was a little scared to talk to him, not having spoken to him since I yelled at him over the phone, so I wasn't sure what was going down. But he was in good spirits, and the conversation was wonderful. We talked about how challenging the show was, how happy we were to have made it through the first season, and how the next season would be even better. He was very upbeat. I thanked him for the opportunity, and said that he could call me again when he knew the next start date, and that I was looking forward to a few days off. He thanked me and left. To me, it sounded like a nice "farewell and see you later" conversation, and I appreciated his kind words. I didn't know he wasn't aware I was leaving, let alone going on to another show.

That was a great last conversation, and I felt that my job had ended on a good note.

I was wrong.

I said goodbye to the two or three people who were in the office, telling them that I'd see them the next time around, including the assistant. It turned out that no one knew I was leaving. I hadn't made an announcement about it, but I had an out date, so it was no big deal. When a job ends, you just go. That's the way of things in a freelancer's world. However, after I left, some phone calls must've been made that ended up reaching Bert, because it turned out he had no idea I was leaving the show. Terry had never spoken to him about it. And I had thought that my last conversation with Bert was a farewell conversation! How could it have gone so wrong?

That afternoon Terry left me a voicemail insisting that I return to work, as if he didn't know that I had another job. I was furious. I left him message telling him as much. But I did go back to the office to talk to Bert. I don't remember why, but it was probably to help smooth out whatever Terry was going through.

I returned to the scene of the crime and sat down in Bert's office. We talked about the fact that he'd had no idea I was leaving. I told him that Terry and I had settled on my out date a very long time ago, and I hadn't thought I needed to run it by him. I also let him know where my next job was and what I would be doing. I remember Bert complimenting me by saying that I was his production cornerstone, and he couldn't do without me. I didn't hold back. I told him that if I was his cornerstone, he wouldn't be paying me a third less than the other production manager. And I said that I'd stay if he matched what the other show was giving me. Of course he back-peddled, telling me he couldn't do that given money constraints. So I wasn't a cornerstone, after all… He was just upset that I had left without his royal blessing.

After the conversation, I went to my old office to pick up a couple of things I'd left behind, and then his assistant needed to put in her two cents. "You're a traitor," she told me. "He gave you a second chance, and this is how you treat him." I'm thinking, *What? Second chance? What does that mean?* He never told me anything about second chances. All he said was that I was his cornerstone. Talk about mixed messages. Apparently, he still didn't like me, and she was loyal to him, so I was the one who was abandoning Bert… and it was personal. That was crap. I was going to another job in order to support myself.

Well, after she berated me, the accountant (the guy who wouldn't advance me any money while I was away) told me that I should have left another way, that I didn't do it right, and how dare I treat the production this way. All I could think about was that I could care less about what he had to say, and I wanted to leave this god-forsaken place at once. But, hindsight being 20/20, I should have gone directly to Bert and not Terry in the first place. It was a good lesson to learn for Terry, and I figured that I had severed my relationship with him forever. But I didn't care. I did it the way normal people do; I had an out date, I asked to leave early, I got permission, and I left. If the execs can't get together and talk, it's not my fault.

In a way, it was a compliment. This jealous behavior from Bert seemed to indicate that on some level he needed me—not enough to pay me more or advance me—but he felt he needed me nonetheless. I left, figuring that I wouldn't be back for the second season, and was moving on to bigger and better things. And I found out they ended up hiring at least three other people to do the job that I had done. So in the end, it cost them more money anyway.

But the whole episode wasn't at an end yet.

I was incredibly excited about my new job. I was hired to be an associate producer on *The Mole*, which was essentially doing what I had been doing on *Amazing Race*, except to my mind, it was a title up since the word "producer" was now in my title. The Mole was an international game show in which the contestants completed tasks together that earned money into a pot that only one of them would win. The Mole was to sabotage the tasks to keep the money low. After each day, there would be a test to determine who would know who "the mole" was. The person who had the worst results of the test was eliminated..

It was great to be working on a different show. What I enjoy most about new jobs and why I like the freelance lifestyle is the excitement of constantly being able to meet and work with new people. It helps you increase the breadth and depth of your experience and also exposes you to different perspectives regarding work. I like making friends and was eager to work with a whole bunch of new people.

My new boss was cool. His name was Tim. He was young, smart, and a real go-getter, and he reminded me of Mark on *Wild Things*. He didn't have reality TV experience, but he had done a lot of other things and the coordinator had experience in commercials. So we all came from different backgrounds. I felt quite lucky to be there.

As I was getting settled into my job, I was to come into a meeting. I figured it was going to be one of those "getting to know you" meetings that producers do at the beginning of every show to welcome people aboard.

I was wrong.

It was a party of sorts, or at least there were a lot of people. There was the producer, the business affairs people for the production company, and an attorney I had met on *Amazing Race* who worked with both ABC and the production company that produced *Amazing Race*. Apparently Bert was accusing the production company of stealing me or doing something illicit to procure my services. I can't imagine what. So I had to go into an account of how I had gotten the job. Simple: I had sent in a resume. That was it. Nobody had solicited me specifically; I had answered an ad on a website. And then the producer said that they'd hired me because of my international experience and my good reputation.

This was similar to what Bert had done to the production manager of *Wild Things*, with one key difference. My contract. Thankfully, the fact that I hadn't signed my contract put the attorney in a difficult position. I told him flat out that *Amazing Race* had no ties to me, that I had given the company an opportunity to hire me (which I had), and they hadn't acted upon it.

While I put a good spin on my situation, and kept a smile on my face, inside I was enraged. I wanted nothing more than to put Bert in his place. I was tired of the crap he kept doling out to me, and this was the last straw. The meeting ended on a positive note, in that I wasn't fired, but I didn't feel confident that the issue was dead and buried. I knew how persistent Bert had been in the past, so when the meeting wrapped up, I called my attorney.

"Line them up." I told him. "If I get fired today, I plan on suing everyone involved in *Amazing Race* and taking all of them down except the production company of *The Mole*. I would never sue them, they're a good company." I was ready to take everyone down with me.

Luckily for Bert, I was not fired, and I did not sue. My career would take a nosedive all by itself. A lawsuit wasn't necessary for that.

CHAPTER 8
WEAR UNDERWEAR TO BED

My anger finally dissipated because no one, at least for the moment, was angling to have me fired. I was busy setting up for the next show, and I didn't have to waste much time thinking about what Bert might ultimately do. But I did have a sort of mental dilemma.

I was really nervous.

Working for Bert was easy, regardless of the drama I went through with him. I knew what to do and how to do things. On this show I was hired as an associate producer, and I figured that my duties would be basically the same as they'd been on *Amazing Race*. But I wanted to figure out the difference between what I had done as a production manager and what I'd be doing as an associate producer. I figured it would emerge as I went along. It's a process I go through with each and every job I do. My friend Laura thinks I'm insane to wallow in doubts because I can do whatever task I'm given, but I always think the worst, telling myself, "Well, if this doesn't work out, I can work at McDonald's." That's right, instead of shooting for the stars, I shoot for my foot. It's a mental battle that eventually goes away. But since the title and salary were a step up, I needed to be better than I had been as a production manager.

But my multitasking ways of the past were going to change. All of the things I did on other shows—getting visas, securing locations, dealing with contestants, dealing with vendors—I didn't have to do on this show. It seemed like such a void. There were other people assigned to many of the tasks I had done in the past. So I was really trying to figure out how to fill my days. And since *The Mole* had already had a first season, many elements were already in place that I might otherwise have needed to figure out myself, like vendors, equipment, and staffing crew. I was actually worried about being busy. Slowing down was not my thing.

One Year of Reality and How It Nearly Killed Me

The first few days at my new job, I just sort of sat at my desk and tried to create tasks for myself. I didn't understand why they'd wanted me to leave *Amazing Race* early if there wasn't much for me to do at the beginning. But I did get to know my co-workers, and I tried to find ways to help them. One of the most interesting times I had at the production office was listening in on conversations that the line producer was having. The walls were thin. I wasn't trying to listen, I didn't have a glass to my ear against the wall, but I could occasionally hear some intense conversations. It never seemed to be going well on his side of the wall.

I was getting sort of claustrophobic from not being bombarded with work like I had been before.

My name is Deborah Wolff and I'm an adrenaline junkie.

I'm addicted to chaos, solving problems, always being in a crushingly tangled moment. Dire circumstances are apparently what I live for, because I was already thinking how bored I was going to be at this new job. Plus I was the outsider. The line producer hired some of his own people, and the show was already staffed, so I didn't have some sort of say in the process as I had in the past. You could say I was not one of his "peeps," and sometimes that can work in your favor, sometimes not. If you aren't part of a group, then you have a better chance of being hung out to dry. On the other hand, if they really need you because they don't have the experience you do, they might look to you for enlightenment and advice. I preferred to think the latter was the case on *The Mole*. This line producer had all the qualities I liked in a person and a boss. He was up front, driven, articulate, and a hard worker. Best of all, he had a good sense of humor. I had to slap my mind awake and stay focused on doing a good job, not worrying about the politics of the show.

And even though I had worked on a couple of reality type shows, I was not prepared for this one. It was closer to feature filmmaking than it was to the run and gun shooting I was used to. Oh, it had the usual crews following contestants, but I never had to deal with lighting up locations, decorating them, or putting out props. I had never hired electricians or grips or any other crew members besides cameramen or soundmen. And, unlike with *Amazing Race*, we didn't run around every day to different countries; instead, we were settled in a few places in two countries. Everything seemed larger about this show, though it was similar in set up to the *Amazing Race*, including the fact that the entire staff would go overseas and set up one huge production office. And that was the big difference. My hotel room wouldn't be a production office this time. We would turn a hotel ballroom into a production office that would house everyone and their equipment so that we could all work in one place and everyone would be in the loop. This was a big deal for me. It was like I finally had breathing space.

As such things usually go, I was in my element within a week, and was ready to confront the challenges of my new job. We had already selected the countries where we'd be going, but one of them changed at the last minute since the hotel we were going to stay at was bombed. I was grateful for the change. We needed to hire some crew in each country. The country that was dumped didn't really have a lot of crew to choose from, so there were many reasons I was grateful we weren't going there.

When the final countries were settled on, Italy and Switzerland, I went about working with the local facilitators who had been hired by the line producer to find overseas crews. We had a German and French crew for Switzerland, and a German, French, and Italian crew for Italy. Some of the German and French crew members stayed with us throughout the entire shoot, as some of them had worked on the previous season, and we used German drivers in Switzerland to drive around the crew. The facilitator for Switzerland was German, so his people came from there as well. The French crew seemed like an odd one to have, since we were not filming in France, but they had worked on the previous season of the show, so it made sense to bring them back. I made the crew member's deals either individually, for department heads, or through the facilitators, for the drivers and production assistants, under the watchful eye of my boss.

Pre-production had started before I arrived on the scene. The segment producers were coming up with ideas for games to make the show intriguing. The contestants were already in the process of being selected, and everyone involved in the show had to wear a badge. The badge was to indicate what level of information you had. My badge meant that I did not know who the mole was. There were only two people who had a badge that said they knew who the mole was, and those were the show's two producers. The mole was the person who would try to sabotage events and information in such a way that none of the other contestants knew who he or she was. Your badge determined which meetings you went to, what paperwork you got, and where you were able to go on the set.

It was my understanding that the producers pre-selected someone to be the mole and took him or her into a room with just the two of them to make the arrangements. If the contestant turned down the opportunity, I don't think he or she would have been on the show. And the mole from the first season was a segment producer or consultant on the second season, which is the one I worked on. There were a couple of games that I had the opportunity to try out, including Blackjack, which is my favorite table game. It was ultimately used on one of the episodes of the show. And if you think of a reality show as a war, we spent the time prior to shooting making battle plans, scheduling shoots, and finalizing ideas. And like every plan or show, it started to look great on paper.

I hung out with the travel department from time to time as they were handling the hotel arrangements and visas for the crew. I gravitated toward them because they were doing work to which I could relate, work I had done in the past. And they were much busier than I ever was. I wanted to help, but they didn't seem to need anything from me. They were preparing the first crew members to arrive in advance of the rest of the team to set up shop. That would be me; Kristen, the head of the travel department; and one of the producers. We were going to Switzerland first.

The staff packed up the office supplies and equipment and shipped it ahead of us so that it would be there when we arrived, and we could get everything set up. The flight was long but pleasant, and we took a beautiful train ride up to the Alps to make it to our final destination, the hotel where we'd be setting up shop. The air was the thinnest I had ever experienced, but it was really fresh and clean. Since it was the off-season, many places were closed. There was no snow but the mountains were a beautiful green with pine trees dotting the landscape as far as the eye could see.

When we arrived, we met our facilitator from Germany. I had only spoken with him briefly once or twice and had some sort of image in my head of him looking like my uncle, 6'7" with curly brown hair, a big guy. But he was much more entertaining than I could ever have imagined.

He was a riot.

I can say this because I'm half German, and I saw characteristics in him that I had always ascribed to that side of my family. He was stern looking, and he had a way of speaking that always made him sound upset or off-putting. I had figured all of that out from my brief conversations with him. But what made him seem so silly was the fact that he always seemed a little "off center" (some would think he was tipsy), and he was wearing what I call a "Swiss Miss" outfit. He had on some kind of overalls, a shirt, and what looked like either long socks or lederhosen. I don't know how to describe the combination beyond saying that he looked like Shirley Temple's grandfather in *Heidi*, only funnier and less put together. I also met his coordinator, whom I liked very much. She was cute, responsible and hardworking, and like me, she wanted to get the job done. I really looked forward to working with her.

But I had a lot to learn.

I had never set up a production office overseas, except in my own hotel room for only a couple of people, so I wasn't sure how to go about it. And while I was aware that they have a different set up for electrical currents overseas, I had no idea that they used differently-sized printer paper in Europe than in the U.S. Can you figure out why that would be? Who said, "We have to be a little different from the Europeans, and we can do that by changing our paper!" I'd like to know the story. We were shipping our own paper to be used in the printer and copier we were getting from the facilitator. If I had known earlier, I would not have shipped office equipment or supplies. Instead,

I kept trying to make the "American" paper work in the European copier. For a couple of critical weeks, I just thought that the copier we had gotten from our facilitator must've been defective, not that the paper was the wrong size. I hate having flashbacks of my stupidity. Oh well, now I know. Ultimately, toward the middle of the shoot, I actually did get a better copier, and I went out and purchased a printer that would work with European paper.

A minor inconvenience compared to what was going to happen to next.

Everyone was starting to arrive, along with the rest of our equipment, and me and Kristen and the rest of the staff who had arrived early were still putting together the production office. The show's executive producers and a couple of network executives also showed up for the first few days of shooting and for the big production meeting where we'd go over everything with the crew and staff. The network execs probably came to make sure everything was okay, or maybe they just wanted a reason to make a trip to a beautiful country. Either way, it was a big deal to have them there.

My boss was disappointed by the sloppiness of the paperwork, particularly the crew handout. It was not a clean handout; it was lopsided and kind of dirty owing to the discrepancy with the paper size, and he was bitterly disappointed.

On top of that, the German crew was getting upset. I spoke to the one German I had been in touch with from the beginning, who had put the rest of the crew together. He was not happy about the rate we were offering for his services and for the rest of the crew. I always deal in flat rates, regardless of cost, and accounting usually backs that number into a twelve-hour day (when timecards are used). I had done all of this on the other shows I had worked on without a problem, even when I dealt with international crews. I mean, everyone wants to make money, but we only had so much budgeted. There wasn't money for additional overtime. But he felt that the deal needed to be for either an eight- or ten-hour day with overtime after that. I told him that was not our deal, and the problem started to spiral from there.

I had to tell the line producer about this new, late breaking development. It was a few days before the shoot, and it wasn't good that this was coming up now. I felt like I had done something wrong. I'm always ready to blame myself first rather than standing up for my actions. I think it's easier to just solve a problem instead of playing the blame game. I would always say, "Just blame me and let's move on." I hated to say that on this one, though, because I knew it would be another disappointment for the line producer. He wanted me to resolve the problem, but the only solution I could come up with was to get another crew, which didn't seem so realistic this late in the game. The Italian crew jumped on the band wagon about overtime as well. So I definitely hadn't made myself clear enough to solve this problem before our arrival.

I'm not sure how the line producer ultimately dealt with this issue from a budget standpoint, but it was another lesson learned. And since we had very, very long days, there would've been overtime anyway. There was no way that twenty-hour days would've been accepted at a flat rate. But then again, I don't think anyone anticipated or wanted twenty-hour days. So either way, they would have to be paid overtime. And I felt that I had to really work hard to make up for that big gaff. Instead of looking forward to the rest of the shoot, from that moment on, I would replay every mistake that I'd made or thought I'd made. My mental game started to get the best (or worst) of me.

One of the most interesting parts of this show was the freebies we were given to use. I hadn't seen this on any shows I had worked on up until that point, but it's what is now called "product placement." We would get something free to use so long as we featured it prominently in the show. We had a few new cars as well as a hundred cell phones. We received these things in exchange for the free publicity generated from using them on air. The cars had to be picked up in Germany, and we had some of the crew go and get them. They were used in the show to transport the ousted contestants, and the execs and crew also used them whenever it was needed. One day, a couple of crew members driving one of the cars got a flat tire. What I remember was that it took a while to get a replacement because the cars had not come out yet, so there weren't any spares available. That's how new these cars were. Everyone used them except for me, since I didn't know how to use a stick shift. Another mistake. The line producer didn't seem too disappointed, but he did say that I should learn how to drive stick for the next international show I did. One night I needed to pass out call sheets for the next day, and someone had to drive me around to all the hotels, none of which were close together, to deliver them. No one is ever happy working late at night, so I had one very upset driver.

Unlike *Amazing Race*, this show was in its second season, which meant that they'd worked out most of the kinks and problems in the first season. The one disadvantage was that most of the production team was not the original production team, so all of us new people were learning as we went. Still, it helped that it had been done before.

The other nice difference between this show and *Amazing Race* was that we had time. Time in one place, time to test out the games, and time to get to know each other and the contestants. Okay, not a *lot* of time, but certainly more than on *Amazing Race*. The two people I immediately hit it off with were the travel team of Kristen and Monica. Kristen had a great production background and Monica was a bit greener, but both of them shared my work ethic. And we just had a connection. We all had a fondness for Aerosmith, and on many a late night when everyone was gone except for the three of us, we would be blast the band's songs out of our computers.

The schedule for the show became brutal in that the hours we needed to put in each day were horribly long. Again, everything looked great on paper until the shoot was executed. There were very few days, if any, when we didn't work more than twelve hours. In fact, most of the time I probably didn't go to bed until midnight or two in the morning, only to get up at 7 a.m. the next day. Thirty days of that sort of schedule would have worn out anyone. But I think that coupled with the last shoot I had done and three years of working on *Wild Things* with only two weeks off, my mental game was off. I was beginning to feel the effects of fatigue. I think that when you're constantly tired, you're like a drunk, by which I mean you let your true feelings out without thinking about it. So if I was mad, I showed it; if I was upset, I said something stupid. I could hear myself doing it, but I couldn't help it. I wasn't myself. Some external force had overtaken my body. But I pressed on.

I tried to have a good sense of humor especially when I was in a dark mood, and overcompensated by trying to do as much as I could for everyone else. A couple of times I unloaded office supplies and equipment essentially on my own so that the other crew members could have a day off. I'd also deliver messages, make calls, or do anything I could think of to put a smile on someone's face, hoping that in some way, the good karma would come back to me. I started to struggle with depression and constantly questioned my value to the production, second-guessing everything I did.

The first production office in Switzerland was set up in a hotel room that looked like an empty theatre space from elementary school, with a raised stage and a large flat space where we set up shop. Along one wall was a "balcony" area where the producers and execs could meet and have some privacy. One time I was looking for a producer, and when I called his cell phone, it turned out that he was in the balcony area. I heard one of the executive producers scream down at me, "Next time look before you spend the money on a call." Now, if my mind had been in the right place, I would've blown that off, but I was greatly offended. I gathered some paperwork for the producer I had called, stormed up to the balcony, gave him his paperwork, and handed the executive producer a nickel. I told him it was for the call and walked away. Later the exec came down to tell me that he'd only been joking. I still didn't back down, and told him it wasn't funny to joke about money in front of hard working people. Yep, it was one of those times when you watch yourself become an idiot.

Not everything was skewed. I did manage to do a few things right. We had a photographer from the network with us who had lost his passport. I helped him arrange to go to the nearest American Embassy to get a replacement, and I spoke with the ambassador's assistant to make sure everything went smoothly. He was grateful, and I was glad to help him out.

I also wrangled a couple of things. We had contestant luggage, a hundred cell phones, and about seven of the new cars. And I was responsible for all of them. The cell phones were badly needed, but it was hard to keep track of them, and even though there was a list and the phones were numbered, people kept swapping them, letting other people borrow them, or losing them. It was particularly confusing when we had to travel between Switzerland and Italy. We had to keep some of the Switzerland numbers as we crossed over, while also attaining Italy numbers for when we arrived. At this point several people, myself included, had two phones. Even I lost one of my phones. The phones that weren't used were kept in my hotel room, and I tried to account for all of them each day. I made people look for the missing phones they'd signed out, but usually it was to no avail. No matter what, a few walked away. A segment producer actually called the number of one of the missing cell phones and yelled at the guy to give it back. It was pretty funny. Out of a hundred, twenty ended up missing and four people admitted to losing them, including myself. So I don't think it was such a horrible loss in the end.

The cars were another matter. The keys for the new cars were constantly being switched around and lost or misplaced. Too many people had keys, and I was ultimately put in charge of them. The network execs and producers kept their keys, and the others were given out as needed. We also had vans that would transport crew and contestants, and we had to keep track of those as well.

One morning I was one van short. I couldn't understand it. I had all the keys accounted for the night before, so to have a set missing put me in a panic, especially since the line producer wanted to use one of the vans to do a run. I looked everywhere, afraid that I had lost the keys or really botched things up. I asked my coordinator. She said she hadn't seen them, and I had the travel people, Kristen and Monica, help me look for them. After a couple of hours it was lunch time, and I still hadn't found them. I had to go to let my boss know. It was just another major disappointment in a long list. I really thought that at this point I would be fired. If he didn't have any respect for me, this would be the clincher.

Just as I was telling him that I had lost the keys and didn't know where they were or how they could've been taken, the coordinator came over to the lunch table and told us that she'd given the keys to one of the guys because the facilitator, who ultimately owned the vehicles, needed the guys to pick some things up from his house. Do a personal run.

I was furious that she had outright lied to me, but there was nothing I could do. I would have to wait for the van.

After that, I tried to find a way to let this person go. She was clearly paying more attention to the drivers and the guys on the trip than she was to her job. I later found out that she was doing more than just hanging out with one of them... But it turned out that I didn't have to fire her. One of our crew members got very sick, and we sent the coordinator to be with this crew member while she was having surgery and recovery. At least it got her out of my hair.

And then I had the contestants' luggage to handle. When a contestant was eliminated at the end of the show, they would be sent to an undisclosed location where they'd stay until the end of shooting. That way no one outside of the crew would know who the mole was if that person came home early from shooting. So when a contestant was eliminated, I would go back to my room, grab his or her bag and hand it off to the attorney, who would debrief the contestant before he or she got on a plane for the undisclosed location. There were quite a few contestants, so I had a lot of luggage in my room. And some of it was really heavy. I didn't go through the bags, but I was certain that there had to be an anvil in at least one of them. There were some pieces that hardly had anything in them. I should've figured that the one bag that was empty must've belonged to the mole, as the mole would never be the one to leave.

The greatest challenge was the moving of the production from one location to another. We had to pack up everything— the office, the video equipment, and the people—and set up at another base. I was responsible for designing the move and figuring out who would be assigned to drive, what would go in each vehicle, and how the equipment would be unloaded.

There are two types of people on a shoot: Those who get overtime and those who don't. Those who get overtime will get a day off to make sure that they don't go into major overtime because they haven't had any breaks. Those who don't get overtime (like me) are expected to work until the job is done because overtime is not an issue. However, the non-overtime people need a break as well, so there were days that we designated as holidays for everyone. Usually the crew would be given the next day off after we moved to a new location. Then they would have to start fresh the day after that. This was a little dilemma, in that the office had to be up and running when everybody returned. So that meant that someone had to set everything up on the day off.

That someone was me.

I would arrange to have a vehicle close to an entrance so that I could unload the production truck and work with the hotel to get all the tables, chairs, and whatnot set up in our office. Unloading was difficult because some of the equipment was heavy and there wasn't always a dolly around. If someone saw that I was unloading everything myself, I would get some help, but I was basically the one setting things up. When we were in Lucca, Italy, though, the Italian crew (I love them) saw me unloading, and they all pitched in to help. I was very grateful. And, of course, after I had set everything up the way I thought best, everyone changed everything, so it was like re-setting the office up all over again, but at least the truck was unloaded. All of the computers had to be rewired to link to the printers and the camera equipment was organized by the crew and had to be set up so that the crews could easily look through their gear. And Kristen made sure there were enough phone lines, electricity and security, so that we would not have anything stolen. So there was a lot to setting up a production office. Imagine your office being torn down and set up in a few hours. A daunting thought.

The segment producers had their hands full. Before leaving for location, they had devised the many games that would be played on *The Mole*, prepped the types of questions that would be asked of the contestants, and figured out where they wanted to shoot. But there were inevitably complications. As each game was being set up, a props list was put together so that someone could go out and get the items needed for that segment. One of the games involved little gnome figures, several of which were needed. Well, there aren't very many gnomes in Italy, and they were hard to find. Everyone was working on finding enough of them—from making calls to stores to just driving around to see if anyone had a gnome decorating their yard. I remember Emanuele, the Italian Facilitator telling me repeatedly, "Deborah, they will not find gnomes here. We don't do gnomes." I would still flip through the phone book in between his protestations that we'd never find anything. So a lot of the details that were needed to make a show work didn't always happen, and they were usually figured out last minute. This event had to be reworked without the use of gnomes.

One day in Lucca, the shoot needed bicycles right away, so I ran out with the line producer and we rented two bikes. Lucca is an enclosed city, and I had trouble reading any of the maps we had. I was constantly getting turned around and lost. The crew was shooting around the outer edge of the city, so the line producer and I rode the bikes around until we found the crew. We dropped them off, and then walked back to the office. We also had an incident in Lucca in which the host, Anderson Cooper, was recognized by tourists as the host of *The Mole*. This was not a good thing, as the production company didn't want anyone to know where we were traveling and didn't want to give out anything that would give anyone an idea of what was going on. Everything had to be hush hush so it would all be revealed when the show was on television. In the end, that never became an issue.

I really liked my boss, the line producer, and had a great deal of respect for him. We actually had common interests, and I remember thinking that he was the male version of me. We both played cello, grew up in the Midwest, and had a dry sense of humor. So it was nice to have someone to relate to. Our first night in Lucca, he was kind enough to take me out to dinner, and we had the chance to really talk about what it's like to work in reality television. I got the sense that it was his first reality show and of course it was my second, but I had a good first one in *Amazing Race*. The waitress was kind enough to give us some free Limoncello. It was nice that she wanted to do that, but it's an awful drink. Still, we drank it and thanked her. The Italian people we met along the way were uniformly very nice and generous, just like the waitress. I was often greeted by a "Hey" or a "Good Morning."

Lucca was toward the end of our shoot. We only had one more production office to set up after that. I decided to buy a proper printer to finish the shoot, one that matched all the European requirements for power and paper.

I have to say that I was kind of sick of the food at this point. That's not to say that the restaurants in Italy weren't fabulous. In fact, one of the drivers introduced us to a wonderful restaurant where they had the best steaks in the world (or at least the best I've tasted so far). Of course, I hadn't thought about mad cow disease; I was just hungry for something American. And every day we had a delicious continental breakfast, but what I was really craving was an Egg McMuffin, Big Mac, fries… Anything McDonalds. So when I saw that Lucca was getting a McDonalds, I counted the days until it opened. We ordered lunch from there on the very first day. And it was just like home. It's really sad when you're in such a beautiful country and you're craving a Big Mac. I could get amazing steaks and beautiful vegetables, the best wine imaginable, and all I could think of was having a Big Mac. When I was home, my go-to quickie breakfast or lunch was McDonald's, so it really gave me a piece of home to have a Big Mac. I was clearly feeling homesick, wanting to do some "nesting" in my new apartment and tell my friends about all the fun stuff I'd been doing.

And by the time we hit Lucca, I was in my element, and had gotten beyond my nervousness about setting up the show. And I had a chance to look around and pay attention to my surroundings. One thing I noticed was that the crew partied a lot. Not outrageous parties, but when I was working late I'd always see the staff outside, dressed up, going out, and having fun. This was not an unusual situation when I was on location. But that could be a personality defect as well. I always gravitate toward working more hours rather than cutting loose and having fun. I noticed that there was coupling up between some of the drivers and some of the female crew. I always tried not to have intimate relationships with crew because of the problems they could pose.

Finally we arrived at our last production office in L'Aquila, Italy, where I thought I would have a happy ending and go home.

We stayed at a hotel owned by Canadians, lovely people who were very helpful and accommodating. This was in July and the line producer organized a 4th of July party with our Italian facilitator. Our German facilitator was there too, since we still had some of his crew and vans with us, and he barbecued. There was food and dancing, and it was a really good time. Of course, I was the party pooper. We had buses take us to the party, and since we were staying at various hotels, everyone had to be dropped off at the right place at the end of the night. Well, people were just getting off anywhere they wanted, and I was trying to get them to sit down and get off in the right places. The crew didn't seem to like me or respect me very much that night, not that I had done anything to deserve that attitude. I was just trying to make sure we didn't lose anyone. After a while I gave up and let it go.

During the entire shoot I hadn't taken a day off. And while I could've slept in or started late, I felt as though I needed to be in the production office early in the morning to make sure everyone knew what was going on and to keep myself in the loop. Shoots would go late into the night, and we would only be able to finish the call sheets and the drivers' schedules once shooting was finished. The drivers needed some turnaround time, and they needed sleep, plus they were not supposed to work outrageous hours according to Italian labor laws. So even after shooting was done, we had to distribute the paperwork on set and at the hotels where the crew was staying to make sure everyone knew what was going on.

Anyway, the line producer told me to take a day off. It sounded mandatory, but I was looking forward to it. Well, the day I would be taking off was after an elimination night, which meant that the shooting went even longer than on a regular day. In the end, I went to bed at 5 a.m. and woke up about noon. I got on a train without knowing where it was headed, and ended up in Florence. I had connected with one of the crew members in the production office (I wasn't sure he wanted me to tag along, but he didn't have a choice—I was following him), and we went to the Duomo. Now, the Duomo was built for very short people, and I am very tall. There are a lot of stairs to climb before getting to the top, and I hit my head a few times on the ceiling and got out of breath from climbing all the stairs. I asked the crew member how many more steps were there, and he said there were only six, so I finished going to the top of the Duomo. It was worth it for the beautiful view of Florence. We also went to see the statue of David, but the line was so long that we didn't end up waiting. We went back to the hotel by train. When we got there, it was raining, but we were picked up by one of my favorite Italian drivers, who brought us to the office so that we could see what was happening.

One day off made up for the one day I didn't sleep.

Another night, we wrapped at 3:30 a.m. I went to my room, put on a night shirt, and quickly fell asleep. I got a call half an hour later.

Deborah this is Marco. (Marco was an Italian PA)
Hey Marco.
Deborah, can we borrow your key to the office?
Sure, why?
There's a fire.
HUH?!?!?!?!?!?!

No sooner had he said that than I dropped my phone and hopped out of bed. In a few seconds I was out of my room, heading downstairs to the room we had set up as an office. I realized after the fact that I was wearing a short night shirt with no underwear and the Italian crew members, who had also heard from Marco about the fire, were following me. I tried to pull my shirt down in the front and the back as I ran down the stairs. Once I got to the doorway, I could see they were trying to break down the door. Marco saw me and took my key, using it to open the door. I believe he was the one who grabbed the fire extinguisher. We entered and turned the corner to see the office area. A huge fire was raging in a small part of the ballroom. It wasn't wide, but the flames were over six feet high and burning right next to all the cameras and equipment. Marco sprayed the office with the fire extinguisher until the fire went out. Not all the cameras were protected with lens covers, and the blue foam had been sprayed all over the office. I was concerned that the cameras might be broken for good. The fire had started from a battery belt that was now completely disintegrated and another battery belt that was next to it was partially melted. I thanked the guys and most of them went back to sleep. I ran upstairs to change.

I called the head technician and told him that there had been a fire and that it looked pretty bad. He said that he'd wake up his crew and check out the gear. Then I called the line producer to let him know that we'd had a little fire and the crews were checking the equipment. Of course we woke up the hotel owners, who seemed surprisingly untroubled that part of their ceiling, floor, and curtain had burned up. Finally with a pair of pants on, I got a couple of mops and a bucket, and I started cleaning up with some other staffers. While the techies were working on the camera equipment, I was cleaning up the blue foam from all over the production equipment and floor. I moved around tables, dusted, and cleaned any computers that had the stuff on them. As people started coming into the office, they would help out with the clean-up too.

When the line producer came in, he was astonished at what the office looked like. He told me that from our conversation, he'd thought it was a minor fire, and that everything was under control. Well, it was a much bigger fire, but everything was under control.

I was told that the fire had been caused by a faulty camera battery, and I had to notify the vendor that the battery was faulty. Several years later, though, I found out that the techs hadn't had the right power aligned for it. There was a switch that would tell the battery whether it was on European or American power. It had been on the wrong mode, which had overloaded the battery, starting the fire. What angers me is that the technician wouldn't admit that a mistake had been made, and all the camera guys probably knew about it.

I wish I could've lied about my mistakes so easily and had them well hidden and protected by a crew, but that never happened because the mistakes I made would affect them. By the afternoon, everything had been cleaned up, and I'm sure the line producer had to notify the production office in Los Angeles and start an insurance claim. I remember the hotel owners telling me that it would not have been a big deal if the place had burned down... They would've loved the insurance money. I guess that's why they weren't too upset. They handled the situation beautifully.

There were other problems toward the end of filming too. The head of our German crew was not a happy guy. He wanted to be paid for his final week right after shooting. Well, that wasn't the policy; people were always paid the following week. I sat down with him and explained that, but he wasn't having any of it. I think he was worried that he'd get ripped off and wouldn't get his final paycheck. That absolutely wasn't going to happen, but I guess he just wanted to be done with the shoot. And when I walked past the German contingent and said hello, they'd just stare at me like I was a comic who was bombing on stage. They also drank a lot, and I remember at our last hotel that there was this purple stain on the first floor of the hotel near the breakfast buffet. Turns out the Germans were pouring unused wine over the edge of their hotel room. I was afraid of going to my room alone at night since I was surrounded by them. I had the Italian accountant walk me to my room once because I really thought I was going to get beaten up by a bunch of drunk crew members who didn't like me.

I did have some fun moments.

Dennis, Emanuele's accountant, would always jokingly accuse me of being "mean" to him. I told him if he didn't like it, he could call my mother. After hearing that a couple of more times, I called my mom and handed Dennis the phone. My mom was in on the fun and after Dennis had spoken to her, handed back the phone to me. She then lectured me about being kinder to Dennis and how he seemed very nice. Now up to this point I never told my mother where I was since the shows locations are confidential. This was the only time I really spoke to my mom for any length of time while on the road. She asked me if I was in a place where they said "Ciao." I told her that I was under a confidentiality agreement and had to go. Right before I hung up, I said "Mom, I gotta go, Ciao." figuring she would get it.

The end of the show was finally within our sights, and there was a final night party where everyone ate and drank and took buses to the airport. A few of us stayed behind. My boss asked me to help wrap the show and go to Rome for a few days. I was ready to help out in any way I could. I had a really fun time with Emanuele and was looking forward to spending time with him and Dennis wrapping up the show.

I couldn't wait to wrap up the show and go home. And, oh yeah, enjoy Rome!

I didn't do much in regards to wrapping. Wrapping a show is basically going over the details and seeing what is outstanding in terms of who needs to be paid, what damages need to be covered, and whether anything's missing. In the corporate world, I guess it would be like ending a business and making sure there are no outstanding legal or financial issues. I was ready to help as needed, but my boss was mainly being generous and allowing me to get some R&R and enjoy my surroundings. At first I didn't get that that's what he was doing, and I thought I'd need to do more. I wanted to help wrap out to make sure there wouldn't be any loose ends. But no one needed me to do anything. I was going crazy. I was ready to work, not relax. I couldn't turn myself off. I tried to hook up with a friend from *Amazing Race*, but he was busy working in Milan. So I spent a lot of time walking around Rome, bored. I was itchy to assist if needed. But I did hang out with a couple of other people who were staying to wrap the show. (I don't know whether they did anything to wrap either.)

Finally the line producer, accountant, and I were flying home. I was still wound up and really tired. Kind of like a zombie. I wasn't particularly energetic, but I was mostly functional. I went into the washroom at the airport to try and wake up, but that didn't seem to work. So I sat down away from everyone and just waited to get on the plane to sleep.

Then something happened that woke me up fast.

A few minutes went by and I heard the announcement that it was time to board. I went to get my ticket, but it was gone. I couldn't find it. I didn't want to tell my boss who was sitting about ten feet in front of me. I was trying to figure out how I was going to pay for a ticket back home. I was absolutely panicked and didn't want to look like an idiot. I decided to retrace my steps to find the ticket. I walked down long hallways, around kiosks and finally went into the bathroom. And there it was, lying on the ground. My ticket was in the middle of the bathroom floor, where at least twenty women were standing around, and no one seemed to have noticed it in the last half hour. I can't tell you how relieved I was. I was swearing at myself, much like a crazy person who talks to himself. I think my boss must have thought I was angry about something, but I couldn't tell him what had just happened.

I was looking forward to my window seat, hoping that I'd be able to rest. Of course, another lady was already sitting in my seat. I kindly asked her to move. She didn't even look at me. I asked her again, thinking that if I spoke English louder, she might understand. I don't know whether or not she did, but she sure wasn't going to move. Then I got angrier and asked her. I wasn't going to take this crap from anyone. Finally a flight attendant helped me, and the woman reluctantly moved to the middle seat and I took the window. This took about ten minutes. On long flights back to Los Angeles, even coach had individual screens to watch movies. It turns out that the screen in the middle was not working at all. So I felt a little bad that the woman next to me didn't have video, but I went to sleep pretty soon afterwards and didn't care. I tried to sleep the whole time and only got up once. I was nauseous most of the time, and was afraid to eat in case I would get sick. I didn't want a repeat of what had happened when I returned from the States the last time. Finally we landed.

Just like before, Kelly picked me up in my car. I was so excited to see her. It was good to be home… for about one day, and then I had to deal with another medical situation.

CHAPTER 9
DO NOT GO TO DINNER WHEN YOU HAVE JUST BROKEN YOUR LEG

Well, it was great to be home again. I still hadn't quite settled into my apartment yet as I had been gone a month for the *Amazing Race* and another month for *The Mole*, so I knew I had some catching up to do.

What's more, I already needed another job. I sent my resume off to another production in hopes of finding one. When I was in between jobs in the past, I had been known to send out seven hundred resumes in one sitting, basically to every production company in Los Angeles with some sort of humorous cover letter to help me stand out from the crowd. This time, I was going for only one job. I didn't have the time or energy to send out seven hundred resumes while I was still working. I also figured that if I didn't get this job, I could spend some time organizing my apartment and do a blitz of job applications if necessary. But for now, my only task was to relax and finish wrapping up my work on the show.

I had arrived on a Thursday and my friend Kelly had organized a spa day for me on Saturday. There's something about being on the road that makes you want to have everything scrubbed, rubbed, and massaged off you. So I was looking forward to spa day. And then later that night, Kelly and I were going to check out the new subway system in downtown LA—the walls were lined with art—and enjoy a fabulous dinner.

Saturday promised to be a fabulous day.

The spa was everything I'd hoped it would be. I had a sea salt scrub, massage, facial—the works. I was relaxed and feeling good about life. I had a beautiful apartment that was bright and sunny in

Santa Monica, where I'd always wanted to live, and I had just spent the day pampering myself. And when I came home, I went into the kitchen for a drink and immediately freaked out.

There were hundreds of ants in my kitchen.

Not just in my kitchen, but on the kitchen floor, on the countertops, in my sink, and inside my pipes. They never made it to the living room next to the kitchen or on the rugs. They were after the water. Apparently, it had been a hot summer in Los Angeles. When I turned on my water after getting back from India, the ants must have sensed it and headed straight for my apartment. And there was just a sea of them. I have an extreme phobia of bugs, so this completely grossed me out to no end. Luckily, I found some ant spray and started spraying all over my kitchen and floor. And then it happened. As soon as I stepped foot in the kitchen, I slipped on some ants and ant spray. And like a baseball player sliding into second base very badly, I slid into the table and chairs in my kitchen. I was in agony, and I screamed for help because I saw my neighbor walking next to the house. My window was open, so I knew he could hear me, but he either ignored me or was deaf to my cries. Not only was I in agony, but at this point I felt like I was in some bad horror movie. Ants were crawling all over my body, but I couldn't get up because my ankle hurt so badly. So I did a zombie-like slide/crawl out of my kitchen onto the carpet in my living room and started rolling around, trying to get those damn ants off of me. If I wasn't covered in ants, you'd think I was on fire the way I was rolling around and hitting myself to make sure I was ant-free. Finally, after a doing that for a while, I got onto my back in the living room and propped my leg on a chair. I could see that it looked nasty and wasn't sure what to do next. I couldn't stand up.

When in doubt, always call your friend. I rolled over to the phone and called Kelly.

We exchanged pleasantries, and she asked me how the spa was. I told her it was great, and then I told her, "I think I'll be late for dinner, and I probably can't take the subway around to see the artwork."

"Why?" she asked.

"Because I think I broke my leg."

"WHAT???"

I told her the story, and she was over in a flash. She's my pit bull, coming in with a serious look, ready to take care of the situation. And when she saw the ants, she gave them a good tongue lashing. I watched as she cleaned up the dead ones and made the kitchen spick and span. I was still on the floor looking up at the ceiling, my foot propped up on the couch seat. Kelly sat on the chair and looked down at me.

"We can't go to dinner," she said emphatically. "We should go to the hospital."

"I can't go to the hospital," I said. "I can't afford it. I can get a doctor to check it out if the swelling doesn't go down."

"Well, we can't go out tonight," she said again.

"No, we're going out," I said emphatically.

Now she was dumbfounded. "We can't go out, you can't even get up. How are you going to get up and when?"

"As soon as I have to go to the bathroom," I told her, completely serious. "I'll be up. I'll figure out a way."

And sure enough, I had to go to the bathroom, and since bladder pain trumps ankle pain, I got up and hopped over to it. I dressed up, keeping my foot wrapped in a sock I had retrieved from a past medical visit, and Kelly and I went out to dinner. It was important to me. I wanted to enjoy American food with my friend, and I was determined that a little ankle sprain wouldn't spoil my evening. I was stubborn, and Kelly was kind enough to oblige me. It was a nice evening, with the exception of my ankle, but I was glad to be out, cleaned up, and home.

I went to the office on Monday to finish up any leftover paperwork, and I put together a detailed memo of what I had done, providing information about where I could be reached if there were any questions. I was still limping and my ankle was completely swollen—a nice blue, purple, yellow, black color. I called my doctor, who referred me to a doctor who dealt with sports injuries. I decided to go see him on Tuesday. I went into the office for a while in the morning, and then was off to the doctor. I waited around for a bit in the waiting room. Everyone in the waiting room had a cast or was in a wheelchair. I felt pretty sure that I wouldn't need either, that they would just give me some pain pills, an ice pack, and call it a day.

I'm glad I'm not a doctor.

One Year of Reality and How It Nearly Killed Me

Well, I finally went into the office and they took some x-rays. It turned out that I had broken my leg above my ankle. At least that's what I think I heard. I never care too much about diagnoses, all I want to know is how long it will take to heal and what I have to do to take care of myself. But I remember the broken leg thing. Then he threw in a slider, "Did you know that you broke your ankle before, a long time ago?"

Well, I knew that I'd *hurt* my ankle before. When I was fourteen, instead of cleaning the house like my mom had asked, I helped out some smaller kids who were building a tree house in the forest behind my house. That seemed like a lot more fun. Anyway, I was on the top of the tree and starting to work on the house when I fell through the floor. Apparently it was big enough to hold a couple of little kids, not one big one. I fell about twenty feet, hitting the trunk on the way down. A couple of nails impaled my leg. Not a fun thing. The kids got a wheelbarrow to put me in because I couldn't stand up. And someone, I'm not sure who, got a hold of my mom, who was working. She met us in the forest and got me into her car and to the doctor.

Luckily my mom worked for radiologists, and I got a little preferential treatment. It turned out that

I had sprained my left leg, and I was on crutches for a couple of months. It wasn't until ten years later when I was in college that my right ankle swelled up and started to hurt. When I went to the doctor on campus, it turned out that I had several small broken bones in my right ankle that hadn't healed well from a very old injury. I could only figure that it had happened when I fell out of that tree. Nothing came of the injury—the swelling went down and I was fine. It seemed like a weird thing, nothing more. Neither the doctor nor I could figure out why now it was swollen, but eventually it went away. I should point out that a little kid in high school had nicknamed me "Grace" because I was as clumsy as a bull in a china shop.

Well, since I had "shattered" my ankle before, the doctor thought it would be a good idea to put my leg in a cast up to my knee and keep it on for six weeks to make sure that everything healed properly, and I didn't have more problems with my ankle. The silver lining was that I was able to pick the color of the cast. And once I had my beautiful blue cast on, I went back to work and told everyone I had been walking on a broken leg for the last three days. It sure made me sound tough. At least the pain went away once I was in the cast. The problem was that it was my right leg that was incapacitated. My doctor gave me a temporary handicap permit so that I could park close to things, but I don't remember him saying that I shouldn't be driving.

What an idiot.

I was driving. I used my cast leg to accelerate. It seemed fine. In hindsight it was idiotic because I couldn't hit the break fast enough, especially since I wasn't trained to drive using both legs. I drove like a blind grandmother for the next couple of months. I was a bit nervous to be wearing the cast when I got a call for an interview. I didn't think I would be hired because of my cast, but I needed the gig, so I drove myself to the interview.

I met with Louise, the line producer for *Fear Factor*. I wasn't familiar with the show, so I called my friend Laura, who told me her kids loved the show. It was a stunt show that had three separate events, with the second event being a strange food challenge. She said it was great and I would like it, which I did. I still had the cast on when I went to my interview, but at least I could park right next to the building because I had that temporary handicap permit. Louise was a woman who was very knowledgeable and strong, and I really liked her. She is what I call an East Coaster, meaning that she was very smart, articulate, and no b.s. I would say that she was a young Katherine Hepburn. She reminded me of Mark from *Wild Things*, and it was refreshing change to work for a woman. We hit it off and I ended up getting the job. I was excited that I wouldn't have any down time between gigs, and could go straight from *The Mole* to *Fear Factor*. The other thing I liked about *Fear Factor* was that it was in Los Angeles. I wouldn't need to do more chaotic traveling anytime soon. I finished out my wrap week and everything was fine.

It was ironic that I would be starting my job on a stunt show in a cast. But at this point, I was feeling good about my career, my life, and my finances. It was all going so well.

I had no complaints, but there were a couple of big shocks in store for me.

CHAPTER 10
THE BEST SHOW I EVER WORKED ON

As careers go, mine was progressing just fine. A bit slowly if I compared myself to my younger colleagues, but it was nice to be moving up and not laterally. I finished my work on *The Mole* on a Thursday and would be starting on *Fear Factor* the following Monday.

But for about half a second, I thought that I might have to back out of the job.

I got an unusual call from one of my mother's friends. This was unusual because I never heard from my mom's friends. But I knew Liz. She was a nurse, and she and my mom had been close for many years. She called to tell me that everything was fine, but my mom was in the hospital for a minor heart condition. My mom's heartbeat had gotten really rapid and wasn't settling down, so she'd needed to go to the emergency room and spend the night at the hospital. She was probably going to be released the next day, so Liz told me there was no need to worry.

As if that were possible! In all the years I'd known my mom, she had only been to the hospital once and that was in the 1970s. She had never had a parking ticket or a traffic violation either. She was like Mary Poppins: "Practically Perfect In Every Way." So I was a little panicked. And it was the first time it wasn't one of my friends calling her and saying, "Everything's fine, but…"

So many things whizzed through my head while Liz and I were on the phone. I didn't totally believe her, for one thing. My mom is great at understating—I learned from the master—so who knew how bad the problem really was. And then there was the fact that I was about to start a job. I don't have the kind of job where I could leave for a couple of days and come back or take vacation days. Those kinds of days needed to happen in between jobs. So if

I needed to do anything, now would be the time. I would have to quit my job if my mother's health problem was serious.

So I hopped on a plane the very next day. It wasn't that easy to hop with a leg cast, but I got some help. Liz picked me up and took me to the hospital, where they were still running tests on my mom. So I hung out in her room for a while until she came back. She was surprised to see me. I told her, "What are you trying to do, show me up? I break my leg; you have to one-up me with a heart condition? Come on!!!"

Well, we spent a couple of days together and I explained to her that if anything else happened, it would have to happen after my job ended in five months. Though that may sound selfish, my mom understood that I wouldn't be able to come back. It turned out that some medication and rest was what she needed, and she would be fine. But I was at the age when I needed to start thinking about my parents aging. Well, just my mom. My dad had died of a heart attack before he was sixty, so my mom was the only worry. To my knowledge, her family had no history of heart conditions, but I had to start thinking about how I would someday take care of my mom, and what role my brother would play. I flew back to Los Angeles, feeling a little conflicted about leaving.

But all of that took a back seat as I went to my first day of work on a brand new show with brand new people. It was very exciting, and everyone was pleasant and on their best behavior. My cast was a point of a discussion, but it certainly didn't hinder me. I did feel like it put me in a weaker leadership position. After all, it was a stunt show. I wasn't doing any stunts myself, of course, but the cast did limit me in terms of what I could do and where I could go on set.

One of the fun things about my job was that I'd be working with location scouts for the first time. Before the show even began shooting, we would check out various locations to see if they'd work for particular stunts. We would be doing this throughout the show, as stunts changed and locations fell through. We had to make sure it would be affordable and safe to set up stunts at the location, and that there would be a place for crew parking and the trucks that were needed to help set up the shoot (everyone drove to location, which would be around fifty to seventy people). The field producers on *Amazing Race* had been the ones who got to go all over the world and check out locations. My task had been to follow up with obtaining the permission to film in the places that were chosen. And on *The Mole*, the facilitators in each country did most of the ground work for the location shooting. I had a lot of fun helping scope out locations.

My first location scouting mission was only a day after I started. We were going to check out an oil rig. I was in my leg cast, but you couldn't see much of it because I had pants on. We took a boat out to the rig, but as soon as I stepped onto it, I was yelled off it by the company supervisors. Because of my cast, I had to stay on the boat while the production team (location manager, producer, director, AD) took a tour of the rig. I didn't like standing out like that, especially not on my second day. While it wasn't my fault, I was embarrassed, and I knew I wasn't earning any brownie points. Soon that humiliating feeling would go away.

I wanted some way of compensating for my temporary disability, and before I knew it, I found an opening. One of the producers would often bring disgusting delicacies to the office in a bag to see if anyone would give them a taste. It was a variety of things, mostly pig parts, uncooked. I usually said, "Sure." When the producer asked how anything tasted, I told him it just needed some salt and pepper, maybe a little sauce, and then I would say it was gross. Most of the food he brought in actually tasted like the smell of the frogs we'd dissected in high school biology class. YUCK! I hated it, but by trying it, I felt like I was proving that I was stronger than the cast on my leg. I didn't think they'd give me anything that would put me in the hospital or cause me to sue them. And I know they made sure that the food was "approved" by someone or some agency.

One time they tried to have the eating of a placenta as part of the B Stunt, which was the second stunt of every show. There would be three stunts, two physical and one food, but the placenta was not approved. I was never involved in how the stunts were structured, but I did taste many of the B Stunts. There were two things I never volunteered for, an insect dinner that was supposed to be spaghetti and meatballs (actually I think it was worms and blood balls) and Balut (almost hatched duck eggs). I knew what Balut was, and thought it was more disgusting than anything I had ever experienced... Still, the *Fear Factor* spaghetti was even grosser. Most of the taste testing for the show was done on a volunteer basis, with the occasional money incentive. It made the office smell really bad at times.

It was a nice distraction to occasionally help the producers by volunteering to eat the food, but I was getting paid to do other things. I did some hiring for the show. Two coordinators were needed, and the line producer had already hired one. The coordinator was a very self-assured, aggressive, and funny woman. I don't mean aggressive in a bad way; she was someone who always questioned things and wanted to figure them out, rather than just passively doing her job. She was definitely production manager material, but she may have needed one or two more shows under her belt before getting that promotion. I had one more coordinator to hire, and I hired a guy whom I felt would work well with the other coordinator as the location coordinator, and a friend whom I'd worked with before as the office coordinator. I wanted to have someone in the office I knew and could rely on. I also had to hire a few production assistants. The executive producer of the show had given me the names of one or two people he wanted me to interview for these positions, but he didn't pressure me into any decisions. I didn't have any problem hiring whoever the producers wanted, though, since they were entry-level positions. Almost anyone could be a PA if they were responsible, took direction well, and volunteered to assist in unexpected ways. I also believe that if the top executive of the show makes a suggestion, you should take it seriously. Other than the PAs, the additional coordinator, and the office coordinator, I didn't need to do any hiring. The show was in its second season, and many of the people who had worked on its first season were back. The line producer was new, as the original line producer was working on a pilot for the same company. The schedule for the show was very simple, it was a six-day work week with three days of shooting, three days of prep, and one day off.

And like every other show I'd worked on as a production manager, the job responsibilities were different. On *Amazing Race* I didn't hire anyone, on *The Mole* I hired some of the crew, and on *Fear Factor* I hired most of my staff. On *Amazing Race* I worked closely with contestants, on *The Mole* I had little interaction with them besides keeping their luggage, and on *Fear Factor* I didn't need to deal with contestants at all except when there were celebrities involved and we wanted everything to run smoothly. On *Amazing Race* I didn't have to deal with day-to-day production issues except when it concerned visas, passports, and sending crew home. On *The Mole* I dealt with issues that couldn't be handled by segment producers. On *Fear Factor*, I supervised the shoots from a production standpoint. I wasn't bored exactly, but I had more down time than I'd had on other shows—my days weren't spent shuttling from one crisis to the next. And I had this weird desire to be totally swamped. Only when I was busy did I feel like I was being successful. I was actually having symptoms of withdrawal from being overworked.

Once we were on the set and shooting, I was enjoying the work and started to feel that familiar rush again. My cast had finally come off before we started shooting, and I was back to normal, although I still volunteered to try the strange food. I spent much of my day in the production trailer taking care of small details, keeping an eye on how things were going, and reporting back to the production office. I enjoyed watching the crew set up the lights and the cameras and seeing everything come together from scratch. It was like the scenes from the movie *The Sting*, when the crew would set up a fake location, and then tear it down in the same day. That's what this crew would do. Show up in the morning, put the set together, including any artwork or lighting that needed to be arranged, set up the cameras and the rigging, shoot the stunt, and then tear it down. It was a long day, but since we only shot three days in a row, we could get some sleep the other three (a little bit).

Working on *Fear Factor* reminded me of working on feature films and not a reality show. So, for me, this was the best show I'd ever worked on, because it was staged, well lit and rehearsed. I had always wanted to work in feature filmmaking; it just so happened that I was making money in reality television. The closest I had come to working on features was assisting the director for a TV movie. Many of my production managing colleagues were glad that they hadn't taken jobs in reality television because of the long hours and poor organization on many of the shows. Features, commercials, and union shows are far more structured and well budgeted than most reality shows. There always seemed to be financial issues with *Fear Factor*, especially in regards to getting additional cameras and crew for the show. I always thought there were way too many cameras, but I wasn't the director or the line producer, so details like that were out of my hands.

One thing that was great about this job, which wasn't true of the other shows I'd worked on, was that we were encouraged not to allow a lot of overtime. It was not the kind of show that needed cameras running or on call 24/7. I did work long days like most of my staff, but not compared to what I'd done on the other shows. For the first time in a few years I was able to get at least eight hours of sleep during the week from time to time. I wasn't used to that.

Another cool thing was that I was finally able to get health insurance. I am a member of the Producers Guild and they offered a health insurance program. So I signed up. The last time I'd had health insurance was on *Wild Things*, as Paramount offered it to their shows after the first season. It was a great thing to have. I was never able to get insurance coverage on my own because I was considered a cancer risk. While in college I had developed a cervical tumor that was only partially removed. Although it was benign, I had been turned down by several health programs because of the tumor, or the monthly payments they'd offered were so high I couldn't afford them. But now I was finally making some money and had the ability to have health insurance. I was grateful. I had taken a real financial hit when I broke my leg, and I couldn't afford for something like that to happen again.

So I was almost an adult. I had a good job, a car, and health insurance. Now I needed to finally start saving some real money and buy a house someday.

I was a freelance person and I needed to make this job last for as long as possible. Since the show was very popular, my goal was to work hard enough and well enough that I would be able to stay on until it was cancelled.

But then the first nail was hammered into my coffin.

First, the line producer who hired me was summarily fired. I wasn't sure why, but my theory was that the line producer who had worked on the show's first season became available, and they wanted him back. Freelance people can be fired at will. I've seen that kind of language in quite a few of my contracts. And even though the executive producer came into the production office to assure us that none of us would be fired, we figured that his guarantee was only good until the end of the season. Then the "new" line producer would probably want to bring in his own team. And in all honesty, I could not fault him for wanting to bring in the people he knew and liked. I could only hope to become so necessary that they wouldn't let me go.

The other nail in my coffin was that I fired one of the production assistants that the executive producer had recommended, and I did it without his knowledge or permission. I'm sure that this particular PA is now a very capable producer or in some other high position. But he wasn't doing the job as capably as we needed; he would frequently fail to finish tasks or else completely forget about them. My office coordinator had many talks with him. But the final straw came when we needed equipment at a distant location and he forgot to pick it up. The coordinator let him go under my instructions. One of the other PAs heard my conversation with the coordinator and alerted the about-to-be-fired PA that he was getting the ax. When the executive producer found out, he was furious (in a nice, calm sort of way, but I could feel the vibe) and told me that he wished that I'd consulted him.

And as it turned out, even though the producer promised that no one would be fired, we had one early casualty.

The office coordinator was a friend and someone I had worked with in the past. We had been on a particularly difficult show together, and I felt that I owed her a good experience, so I'd been happy to hire her. When I was in the office, I felt she did her job, and I figured she was equally capable when I was away from the office. However, one night after a shoot, the new line producer asked me into his office and told me that he was not pleased with her work. I reminded him of what the producer had said to us—that we would all be able to keep our jobs—but he was not dissuaded. And in truth, I'm not sure how effective I was at trying to convince him to keep her. I certainly didn't threaten to walk out if he fired her. At that point, I figured I was on my way out in a matter of weeks anyway. I asked to be in the room when he fired her, but he told me no and asked me to send her in.

I walked back to the production bullpen. It was after 7:00 p.m., and everyone was in the office—the location coordinators, the assistant coordinator, and me. When I told the office coordinator that the line producer wanted to see her, she knew what it was about. She even said to me and everyone else in the room, "What, am I going to be fired?" A few minutes later she burst out of his office. She was very angry with me for not sticking up for her, and she left with a lot of anger. I felt bad, but there was nothing I could have done. I figured at that point our friendship was pretty much over. The assistant office coordinator spoke up and defended me, but my friend wouldn't hear any of it. It was a long time before we spoke to each other again.

Being freelance can be difficult: You can be fired at will, and you don't have any sort of 401K plan or insurance from your company. That's not unique to reality television. What is unique is that most of the shows are not union. *Fear Factor* was the only show I'd been on that had any union presence. The stunts had to be tested, and the people who assisted the contestants were all professional stunt people (primarily from feature films), so the show was an AFTRA show for these performers. And while the rest of the show was not union, most people were treated in a union way and were given overtime for additional hours.

Because I was a supervisor though, I was paid a flat rate regardless of my hours.

Reality shows had not been unionized like scripted shows, which is one reason why there are so many reality shows—they can be made for less than scripted shows. So when a union rep visited our location one day to solicit for joining the union, I notified the line producer. The union rep told me that a union would be good for me because I would make more reasonable wages. I told him that while that was true, it would cost a fortune to be a member, and even then I would have to maintain a certain work load to keep any health insurance, which was the only reason I'd want to be in a union as it was way too expensive. Ultimately, I heard that *Fear Factor* went union for many positions in later seasons. Looking back now, I think that unions would be good for reality TV, if only to keep producers from abusing hourly rates and long work hours. Sometimes being non-union is synonymous with saving money at the cost of the crew.

Shooting did not stop as a result of the union reps coming in for a visit. I continued my work and had to deal with a new situation…injuries on set.

The coordinators and I had all taken an OSHA (Occupational Health and Safety Administration designed to keep people safe in the workplace) course on safety. This was important because we wanted to make the set as safe as possible. I was the safety officer on the set, and it was my job to make sure that pathways and walkways were smooth, there were no poorly placed objects that could cause an accident, and people were working in a safe manner. This was new to me, since there had never been a safety officer on any of my other shoots. On *Wild Things*, one of the crew members had a recurrence of malaria, but other than that, we were pretty fortunate in that we didn't have many injuries, particularly given the fact that elephants chased a car down in Tanzania and a crew had a nasty encounter with some armed poachers in Kenya.

Since it was a stunt show, I figured that we would probably have some injured contestants. This did happen a couple of times, and I remember one occasion when a contestant had to ride a bike across two buildings. He fell midway through and hit a wall. That wasn't supposed to happen, and the stunt had been tested without a problem. But at the last minute, they lengthened the rope which was attached to the contestant. That was part of the reason why he'd hit the wall, but thankfully he was okay.

As it turned out, only two people were injured enough on the set to need hospital attention during my time on *Fear Factor*. The first was the head PA.

The head PA had been recommended by the first AD. They must've worked on something together in the past. I couldn't have asked for a more wonderful colleague. She was tough and a real go-getter; she was always running around set to get things done. I had a lot of respect for her. The day she was injured, we were filming down by a lake. I had checked the area for safety issues, and people were moving around stones and brush so that there was a clear walkway to the lake. When the contestants showed up at this location, they were blindfolded because we were going to surprise them, both with where they were and with what they were going to do. Well, when the contestants got out of the car, they held one another's hands and were led, in tow, by the casting person. The head PA was behind them to make sure they didn't trip or fall. Well, they were going underneath some trees and one of the contestants swept aside a branch as she was passing underneath a tree. That branch whipped right into the PA's face, and she was in an enormous amount of pain.

I left the location with her immediately and brought her to the hospital. It turned out that she had a broken nose. Not something she'd expected, but she was going to be fine after a couple of days off and some painkillers. I always try to inject a little humor into painful situations, and I know she appreciated it that day. And if I'm not mistaken, someone had to drive her car home because she was not in a position to drive. While it was bad, it turned out that she was going to be okay. And being the safety officer, I notified everyone who needed to be notified and did all the paperwork that needed to be done, ensuring that the report at the end of the day reflected the injury. That was the first time I'd ever needed to write up an injury. As it turned out, it was the last.

On a lighter note, we all looked forward to the day when we had Celebrity Fear Factor. Donnie Osmond, Brooke Burns, Coolio, Joanie Laurer, Kelly Preston, and David Hasselhoff were on that episode, and Coolio and Donny Osmond were the two finalists. I couldn't help but root for Donny, who was a fierce competitor and a childhood favorite of mine, but Coolio was definitely in shape and very ripped. A few of us went up to Donny and wished him luck, telling him we were on his side. But apparently that was a violation of the rules. No betting and that sort

One Year of Reality and How It Nearly Killed Me

of thing. So the producer had to send out a memo telling us not to do that kind of thing again. Oh well, another thing for the producer to be annoyed with me about.

If I was keeping score, it seemed to me that I'd done more to annoy the producer than please him at that point. So I tried to lay low and finish out the show, learning all I could from what was going on around me.

Meanwhile, I continued to do some more taste testing. I tried quite a few things, but I never did eat bugs. The assistant director on the show tried worse stuff then I ever would. Even so, I tried different pig and cow parts and a one-hundred-year-old egg. If you can imagine eating something that tastes like a combination of sulfur and your high school biology experiment and has the texture of an old tire, then you have a pretty good idea of what it's like to eat a one-hundred-year-old egg. I tried the egg on location right before they were going to do the actual stunt. The producers needed to time how long it could take someone to eat the egg. There weren't any volunteers. I remember saying that I would do it if I could keep my job, since I knew it was just a matter of time at that point. There was definitely a pregnant pause, but I tasted the egg anyway. It was absolutely gross. I wanted to spit it out, but I heard the producer say that I couldn't. So I pressed both my hands on my mouth and forced myself to swallow the thing. I believe it took twenty-five or thirty seconds to eat that horrible treat. Eggs like this can be found in the "dessert" aisle of Chinese grocery stores. Yuck. I hated it, but I ate it.

One of the more fun taste tests was the habanera pepper. Fun because it was going to be videotaped, and I really wanted to pass the challenge and defeat the pepper. It's worth mentioning that I am not a spicy food eater. I ate that small, innocuous looking pepper and stared down the camera for what seemed like several minutes, probably more like several seconds. I fought to maintain my concentration without reacting, though I could feel myself burning up. It felt as if my head was filling with helium and about to explode. The staff's cheers in the background only made it worse. Finally, I broke my concentration and immediately went for some water, which didn't much help. The burning just went down my windpipe. For the rest of the day I felt like my chest was in the middle of a raging forest fire.

Then came my final taste test—I tried the "blender of fear" for the World Wrestling episode.

Kelly and I were planning a trip to Vegas for New Year's Eve during my Christmas break from the show. I had never been to Vegas on New Year's Eve and was looking forward to bringing in the New Year in a big way. It had been a year filled with hard, rewarding work, and I wanted to celebrate. I knew Kelly was in a money crunch, and I found out that the show was paying to have people test the "blender of fear." I told her to come on down to the office so that we could be taste testers together. Figuring it would be an easy hundred bucks, she agreed.

It turned out not to be so easy...

Blender of fear was a concoction that started with pig's brain, and then we had to roll the dice to see what other two ingredients would be added to it. I went second, which turned out to be a good strategic move. I rolled the dice and the next two ingredients added in were cow's eyes and bile. And yes, I saw them go into the blender, and all of it was mixed together. It was a good-sized glass, not small at all. I could smell the stench of it, so I held my nose and drank the thing. And I received my hundred dollars. There were about six or seven volunteers. By the time the fourth person volunteered, the smell of formaldehyde spread throughout the room and the entire office. Kelly decided the drink was far worse than she'd ever imagined, so she didn't do the stunt and didn't get her hundred. Oh well, we tried. But at least I had a hundred bucks.

Not only was it almost Christmas break, which meant only a few weeks were left before the end of the season, but it was almost my birthday as well. And it was a nice gesture when my staff gave me a gift certificate to a spa. One of the coordinators also wanted me to know that the line producer had contributed the lion's share of the money toward the certificate. I was really shocked. I hadn't realized how generous he was. Everyone asked me what I was planning to do for my birthday. I wasn't planning on doing anything (my birthday was on a Tuesday that year), but I told them that I was planning to sleep through the weekend, if possible.

What happened the next day ensured that I'd get my wish.

Two people were injured on the show that season. The first was the PA, and the second was me.

We were filming a WWE Fear Factor. The second day was the taste-testing day, when the blender of fear would be making its debut. I was looking forward to it because I'd been able to hire a cameraman friend of mine at the last moment. I hadn't seen him since *Amazing Race*, and I was excited to catch up. The location where we were shooting was downtown Los Angeles in a small dance hall. Because there wasn't too much space, the cars were parked a block or so away and the catering truck was a little farther. My usual routine was to check out the location in the morning for safety issues, and then get some breakfast. It was around 6:30 in the morning. There was some hustle and bustle in downtown L.A. that early, but I was concentrating on the preparations for the day. I crossed the street and made my way to the catering truck. I noticed that it was nice to walk on a newly paved sidewalk since most of the roads and streets were always torn up or a mess. But on that day, the sidewalk looked new and was very smooth. I then started flipping through my paperwork to see the schedule for the day.

Then, like a movie, my life went into slow motion… I was about to be face up on pavement questioning my life.

My ankle twisted. I don't know why or how, but it just twisted out from underneath me. Normally you just twist and fall. But I fought the fall and started to twist around myself, struggling to stay upright. I was also carrying my binder and a few other things and was trying not to drop them. I stayed up for what seemed like a few minutes, but then I fell. All I remember is that I ended up on my back looking up to the sky. Normally I could get up from a fall, but this was different. I was in excruciating pain. My right arm felt like it had been shot off. I looked over to my right and saw that my arm was twisted the wrong way, and I knew I was in trouble. My knee was on fire and my whole left side felt like it had been hit by a car. I started to yell for help, but no one was stopping. After what seemed like several minutes of just crying for help, I finally said, "Somebody in catering, HELP!"

I didn't know how close I was to the catering truck, but I was a lot closer to that than anything else from the shoot. And at this point the pain had taken over everything. I just wanted help from anyone. A couple of my crew finally ran over to me and saw that I was on the ground crying for help. One of the more humorous aspects of the situation, as I was told later, was that one of the PAs saw me on the ground and immediately called into our second assistant director to tell him that I was hurt and yelling for help. The second AD immediately ran over to the PA, and the PA pointed down the street, telling him that I was about a block away. The second AD thought it was a little stupid of the PA not to have done anything, but I guess the guy didn't want to get involved. The coordinator let the line producer know that I had been hurt, and the crew was starting to help me out. I don't remember much about the whole situation, but I do remember that there wasn't a medic around at the time. The medic was primarily responsible for the injuries of the contestants. And on the days when we were filming an eating stunt, we saved a bit of money by having the medic come in at the same time as the contestants.

I kept saying things like "Oh, the line producer is going to be so mad;" "Oh my God, I can't believe this;" "Get one of the bad PAs to help me out, and everyone should go back to work." One of the PAs put a furniture blanket around me. I kept telling him nicely to take it off, until I finally snapped and said, "Take that #$###@# thing off me!" He was trying to keep me warm, but I was already on fire with all the pain.

Then, to add comedy to injury, the paramedics arrived. First of all, they wanted to assess my situation, which meant they needed to look at my arm. I didn't want them to look at my arm, because it would mean either taking off my jacket, which would be extremely painful, or cutting the arm off it. It was my favorite jacket, and I didn't want that to happen.

I kept telling the paramedic that I didn't want him to ruin my jacket, and I actually remember crying when he did it. I was waiting on medication, and no one had given me any. I kept asking for it, but all I heard was a discussion between the paramedic and the coordinator about where to send me. "Can you take her to Cedar Sinai?" she asked. "No" they said. "Well, don't take her to County!" After hearing all of this, I said something like, "Just take me $^&#W*@ somewhere and give me some morphine."

While all of this was going on, my life flashed before my eyes. I had no idea what was happening, no idea what I was going to do. I knew I didn't have enough money to pay for the ambulance, let alone emergency care. My health insurance plan had been abruptly cancelled a few weeks before from the Producers Guild, so I was now without insurance. I didn't think about it being a work related injury at all; I felt like I was going to be responsible for all the costs. So much for having a new car and a more expensive apartment! I envisioned myself being literally thrown out onto the streets.

Finally they put me in the ambulance (still with no medication) and off we went to the hospital. And given the city roads in Los Angeles, it was a very bouncy, incredibly painful ride. Each bump was like a knife in my right elbow and left knee. I just kept saying, "God, oh God." The pain was crazy; *I* was crazy. Finally we hit the emergency room, and I got some medication. Someone asked me where the pain was and I told them that my arm and knee were hurting the most. Then I remember a nurse or someone saying, "Should I give her something to not remember?" Meaning that they'd knock me out, but not put me under. And I guess that's when they relocated my elbow (it had been severely dislocated) and took x-rays and such. The PA (the girl who had previously broken her nose) later told me that I was screaming at the top of my lungs, and you could hear me outside of the emergency room. The next thing I remember was that they told me I was ready to go. I asked them about my knee. They hadn't taken a look at it yet, so I went in for more tests before leaving.

I was totally groggy and out of it. I remember four Hispanic men helping me to the bathroom before I was discharged. Turns out it was actually the PA helping me, so you know that the drugs were working.

During all that drama, someone found my cell phone and called my friend Kelly to let her know what had happened. She was a good person for them to have called since she didn't have a regular 9-5 job, and was able to help me. A PA drove me home, and Kelly met me there. I was still a little out of it. Later someone brought my car back to my apartment as well. In the meantime, I had a half-cast on my elbow, a can of soda, and some pills to get me through the day. Kelly went and picked up the rest of my prescriptions. I was too out of it to cry, but I was crying on the inside, scared to death of what was going to happen next. I had no idea what I would do.

I'm sure at some point Kelly called my mom and said something like, "Everything's okay, but…" But I couldn't think about much or even calling my mom. I sat in my rocker/recliner and passed out. My birthday was on Tuesday, and I was injured on Thursday. So I did, in fact, sleep through the weekend.

I realized on Friday that I didn't have my glasses. The drugs were truly working as I didn't realize I could not see anything. I have a really strong prescription. I called the production office but the co-ordinators were busy trying to handle everything in my absence, so I knew they were annoyed that they had to pull someone to get me my glasses. Also, the day I was injured one of the PAs had left the day's filming in my car, so for a whole day, no one knew where the tapes were until someone figured it out.

I was unintentionally causing all sorts of trouble. The show had gotten extended for a few episodes as well, so I was excited to have a job for at least a couple of extra months. I was determined to get back to work as quickly as possible. I had to keep working; I couldn't stop now.

The day after my accident, Kelly took me to the doctor, who asked me to list all my pains. I had pain in my right elbow, left knee, left ankle (the one that had been twisted), left hand, and the outside of my left thigh was numb. They needed to take x-rays of everything. It was a very painful experience, because they try to put you in positions that aren't remotely natural. I was glad when the x-rays were finished. It was clear that I'd need surgery on my elbow, so they wrapped it up in a half cast. They gave me some prescriptions and told me that I could go back to work in a few days. Then we could figure out when I would have the surgery. The rest of the injuries needed to be closely observed too.

Now more than ever I needed to prove that I could survive this accident and work on the show.

CHAPTER 11
THE BEST INJURIES I'VE EVER HAD OR GIVE ME SOME MORPHINE!

I have been injured several times. I remember breaking my arm while in the middle of a roller derby when I was twelve (I was tripped and hit by the opposition and went flying off the rink). When I was little, I ran into a television set and hit my head. I was also injured when I fell after climbing on top of a garbage can, catching part of my thigh. Then, of course, I sprained my ankle falling out of that tree. Once, I had a car accident that was so bad I had to crawl out from underneath the steering wheel (something that wasn't easy for someone my height).

One Year of Reality and How It Nearly Killed Me

All in all, I have some great stitches and scars that tell relatively stupid stories. After the incident while I was working at *Fear Factor*, I had many more stupid injuries to add to my collection. No, they hadn't been earned honorably in battle, but some of my colleagues told me that I should at least embellish what had happened. I could say that I'd been injured in the shark tank or while testing a dangerous stunt. Anything other than that I fell while walking to the catering truck to get breakfast.

When I arrived at work on the Tuesday morning following my accident, they were having a fire drill. My colleagues were hanging around the parking lot waiting to go back into the office. So for a brief moment, I fantasized that I was in a ticker tape parade as a hero returning from war. I emerged from my car, wearing my half cast on my right arm and using my cane in my left hand. I wanted to work at the same pace and act as if everything was normal. But I did have some restrictions that the most daunting of which was that I couldn't write very well. I'm right handed, and it was painful to tense up my fingers and hand to write because my elbow was killing me. So I had to use my left hand. And the only way I had ever written with my left hand was backwards. So every time I wrote something, my notes were backwards and right to left, not left to right.

At least I could type with minimal pain. I'm not one to take a lot of pain killers unless pain is paralyzing me. Luckily Christmas was coming up soon. We all needed the break, since we had worked very long hours up until Christmas Eve.

Everyone felt bad for me, and I was pretty much trying to laugh it off. I do remember the medic and I talked about what had happened. He told me that if he'd been there, he would've given me some morphine. I remember that the medics didn't give me anything even though I was in excruciating pain. There was one shining light at the end of this tunnel.

I was excited for my New Year's Eve plans.

I love New Years. I generally don't celebrate it because many of my friends don't—usually we would just sort of hang out and watch MTV. But this year Kelly and I were going to Vegas, and we weren't about to cancel our plans because of my condition. Another friend of Kelly's was joining us as well, so it seemed as though we would have a fun threesome. I made hotel arrangements as well as dinner reservations at a really fabulous restaurant at the Venetian. It was expensive because it was New Year's Eve, but I knew it was going to be worth it. I just wanted to party.

While I was finishing my work before Christmas break, I found out my elbow surgery was on January 8th. I figured that I'd get a cast and could be back at work within a couple of days to finish the final episodes. It was my goal, but I knew even then that it wouldn't necessarily be a smart thing to do. All I could think about was finishing the job, though. I had to finish the job. The line producer was fine with all of this. He didn't question my resolve when I assured him that I was committed to finishing the shoots.

Also, we got some SWAG for the holidays. The network gave us really nice jackets with the NBC logo in red, white, and blue (in memory of 9/11). We could order shirts and whatnot as well. Well, since I was earning some dough, I bought shirts and jackets and hats for my aunts, uncles, cousins, and second cousins on my mom's side of the family. I ended up spending Christmas with my Uncle and his family, and it was really cool that my entire family had *Fear Factor* gear. All of my little cousins were curious about my cast. I was too, so my little cousin and I unwrapped my elbow and removed it to see what my arm looked like.

I thought I was going to throw up.

Now I'm not grossed out by anything (clearly), but my arm looked really grotesque. It was pure black from the middle of my upper arm to halfway between my elbow and wrist. And there were flashes of red in there as well. I was staring at it like you stare at a dead person. I don't think I realized just how bad my injury was until I actually looked at my arm. Lisa, my cousin's wife (and a great mom-nurse) helped me wrap up the cast again to cover it.

I couldn't wait for New Year's Eve. Since 9/11 had happened so recently, I knew that we'd have to go through a lot of checkpoints, and it would take time. However, I needed assistance getting around the airport and security breezed us through without any problems. That was the only cool thing about having an arm cast and looking like I was in chronic pain—I got first class treatment. We were the first ones on the plane, and in Vegas, someone from the airport met us and whisked us through the airport so that we could get a taxi right away. No standing in the long lines waiting around. Since there were three of us and only two beds, I took a cot in the living room of our hotel. Not the most comfortable, but I figured I'd be the one up all night gambling. If I'm in Vegas for the weekend, I don't sleep. This wasn't my first trip, but it was my first New Year's Eve trip.

Then something interesting happened.

I went into the Barbary Coast to play a little blackjack before we went to dinner. As I was walking to a table I heard, "Hey Deborah! Deborah!" This was the second time something like this had happened to me—where someone calls your name in a big city full of a million people. The first time was at Chicago O'Hare Airport, when I ran into a father of a friend. The odds of running into someone you know in such a big place are so slim. Who could know me in such a big town? I turned around to see a couple of the contestants from the *Amazing Race* season I had worked on, as well as one of the casting associates. Well, I thought that was pretty amazing. We had a drink and rehashed old times and caught up on what they were doing. It was great to see them all again and good to know that they were doing well. But another thought ran through my mind. I needed to call my old production manager buddy, Philip, on *Amazing Race* to let him know that there were some old contestants in Vegas.

I knew that the next race was going to start in Las Vegas. I wasn't sure whether or not it was a coincidence that the old contestants were there, but I wanted to give my friend a heads up. It's ironic that I knew the starting location of the race, which was supposed to be secret, but I guess it was one of those widely known secrets. The contestants were probably the only ones in Hollywood who didn't know where the race was going to start. And I hadn't even learned it from any of my friends who worked on the show; someone had mentioned it to me at a party. So when I called Philip, he was shocked that I even knew. I told him about the situation, and he thanked me for the information. I never saw the contestants again, and I was assured that they weren't going to be a problem in Vegas.

Now I was getting hungry and looking forward to eating at the Venetian and celebrating New Year's Eve in style. I went back to the room to change and get dressed up. Kelly is a beautiful woman, and it doesn't take much to make her look gorgeous. Her friend was also well dressed and very beautiful. I tried to match all their good looks, but I was dressed more comfortably in a baggy shirt that would help hide the cast on my arm and the fact that I was still walking with a cane. So I looked more like the walking wounded than a class act. But I would not be deterred. I hobbled my way to the Venetian.

It was an expensive dinner, something like a thousand dollars for the three of us. But that included champagne that was passed around for a toast at midnight. It was a seven-course delight. We had foie gras, lobster, salad and a number of things I didn't recognize. I even pretended to know something about wine and had a conversation with a sommelier about which Shiraz would go with our dinner. When midnight struck, we walked outside of the restaurant and watched three different fireworks shows. We were in the best place in town to celebrate. A local TV station was also ringing in the New Year live on the restaurant veranda. It couldn't have been more magical.

And then we had to walk back to the hotel.

I didn't think much of walking back; after all, it was a lovely evening. But there was one big problem. The streets and some of the sidewalks had been roped off, and police officers were standing in the middle of the road to prevent people from crossing. You had to go with the flow of the crowd. It was a big crowd, and we were getting pushed around. Luckily Kelly and I are both tall, and I could see her kind of behind me. But people kept shoving into my arm, which was very painful. Kelly started getting freaked out because some guy was really hitting her hard. She has an aversion to crowds, and it was starting to get her in a bad way. I couldn't reach her, but I knew what I *could* do… I raised my cane above the crowd and hit the guy over the head until he stopped ramming into her.

Finally I got to the street side of the sidewalk and approached a police officer. I saw that some people were being allowed to cross the street, so I figured I would ask him to let me go since I was clearly impaired. He refused. I told him that I was getting hurt in the crowd. He still said, "No." I asked him why other people, who were in better shape than I was, were crossing the street. He told me that only certain people who needed to cross were allowed. I told him, "What do you think I am?" I showed him my cast and cane, but he still wouldn't help us. Finally we were able to make it back to the hotel. We were all tired, but I hadn't had a chance to do any real gambling. So I changed into some more comfortable clothes and headed out on my own, looking for a good blackjack table.

I was being followed.

I always walk around everywhere without fear, and while I have a purse, I carry everything valuable in my bra. I always joke that no one's been in my bra since 1985, and I'd kill anyone who tried! But there was definitely a guy walking behind me. It started to remind me of the early morning in Tunisia walking to the coliseum. I could hear his footsteps matching mine. It was late now, and there wasn't much of a crowd around me as I walked to Bally's. The only people on the sidewalk were me and this guy. So I was trying to figure out what to do if he rushed me. After all, I must have looked like easy pickins because of the cane and the cast. I hadn't felt so vulnerable since I was on *Amazing Race*, except this time I felt the danger more strongly. I stopped and played a little bit with my cane, swinging it around. Trying to be surreptitious, I turned to take a look at the guy who was following me. He walked around me, and I watched as he continued down the street. I was relieved, but then I wondered if he had truly been after me or if I'd just been imagining things. I didn't like acting like a drama queen. Oh well, better safe than sorry. Now I could go into Bally's and lose the money from my bra at the casino.

We flew back the next day. I couldn't have had a better time. But the airport was a nightmare this time around. There was a huge line for security, so we looked for someone to help us since I had my injury. We found a security person who took me through in a wheelchair, my friends following behind us with a couple of other people, and we whisked past the long lines and got to our gate in plenty of time.

Before I knew it, I was back at work, but only for a few days because the next Tuesday I was going to have my elbow surgery. They needed to remove the radial head and the bone fragments that had been shot through my arm like bullets when I fell. Again, I reiterated to the line producer that I would have the surgery on Tuesday and be back on Thursday, no problem. I didn't have a choice—I needed to work. I needed an income to pay my hospital bills (or so I thought). On the Monday before the surgery I worked hard to have everything in order so that I would not be missed. Everyone was very supportive and the line producer was especially kind. I couldn't have had a better send off.

The next morning, Kelly drove me to the hospital, and we waited around. It was early, and I could see that she was kind of jumpy. It wasn't long before they were ready to take me back, and she wasn't going to stay around while I was in surgery. I was going to ask her to keep my cell phone in case I got any calls, but I took it with me instead. I asked the nurse if they could make sure I had my phone in recovery in case it rang. I actually thought someone in the office would call me with questions. I know I wouldn't let anyone call if I was in the office, but I always wanted to be available. I saw the doctor, met the anesthesiologist, and that's all I remember.

I don't even remember waking up in a recovery room.

But I did have a dream.

I dreamt that I was lying unconscious in recovery while the two doctors who worked on me were talking.

"Well, it doesn't look good."

"I agree. It would be a miracle if she could use her arm again."

And the whole time I was panicking and having this dream, my body was perfectly still because I was knocked out. Finally I woke up. I was in a private room (or a room that only had me in it). The nurse was checking my I.V., and she greeted me and told me how to get more pain medication with the morphine drip. Everything was all a little fuzzy, but as soon as I learned how to get more medication, I kept hitting the button. I was in a lot of pain and very uncomfortable. In the back of my mind, I kept returning to the horrible truth—I was only going to stay overnight before being released, and then I'd have to be back at work the next day. I heard my cell phone. The nurse or doctor had left it on my chest, just as I'd asked. It was the office. For a split second, I thought I was going to be asked a question, that I was actually irreplaceable because they had needed to call me just out of surgery.

"What are you doing answering your phone?" asked the coordinator. I don't remember what I told her, but it was probably something about wanting to be available. She was just checking how everything went. I told her I was fine. I don't remember if it was during that phone call or later, but I did call my line producer to tell him that I would not be back. I'm sure I was still a little drugged up. But my bad dream had made me realize that I had to focus on my health and not on the show. He was gracious. I felt bad because I had made such a big deal about coming back, but I'm sure he wasn't too surprised.

A few of my friends had shown up to visit me. I could hear them and respond to them, but I didn't feel normal. I kept hearing them saying that I was sleeping, and I would tell them that I was awake. They were having some strange conversations that I will leave it to them to remember. What I do recall was that Kathy, one of my friends from *Wild Things*, asked me if I wanted anything. I told her that I wanted red Jell-O. And as soon as I said that, she went on a search for some. I think I heard that she went into the cafeteria and stirred them up a bit to find it. She was a mom, and it felt great for her to mother me a bit.

That is when reality really hit me.

I had the surgery, and I went home. While I wasn't overwhelmed at the moment, I did have a lot to think about. I was receiving disability, and I'd finally figured out that it was a worker's comp injury, which took some of the financial pressure off my shoulders. Still, the money wasn't much more than you'd get with unemployment, and I think everyone knows that unemployment doesn't cover much of anything. I had to start physical therapy on my elbow and my knee, and I had to see a hand specialist, since I had injured my hand as well. I had to take it one body part and one surgery at a time. Since my income was very minimal, I had to find ways to cut back or earn more money. After all, I had just bought a car a year ago, and I had moved into a more expensive apartment. I had some money stashed away, a 401K from a previous full-time job, and a small mountain of credit card debt. But what I was bringing home wasn't going to pay all the bills. Sure, workers comp took care of the surgeries, therapy, and drugs, but the day-to-day stuff was my responsibility. I really regretted not having disability insurance. Obviously this was the reason to have it.

But the biggest hurdle for me to overcome was my elbow.

I still had it in a cast after surgery when I went to my hairdresser to get my hair done. This was the third time I had seen her; each time, I had some new cast or wrap or scar to show her. She wouldn't have been able to recognize me without all of my injuries.

I couldn't sleep in my bed. It was too uncomfortable to rest on my side, my left knee still hurt, and my right elbow was constantly in pain. So I began to sleep, live, and breathe in my recliner. I did all the physical therapy the doctors asked me to do, but the biggest thing I did was hold onto the arms of my recliner and lean back, stretching my arms. My goal was to re-acclimate myself to straightening my elbow, as it had "hardened" into the L shape it had been in for a while. For hours I would sit in the chair and just stretch it. It was extremely painful, and a couple of times I thought I'd really screwed up my elbow. To this day I still stretch it out because it can get pretty stiff. But I wasn't out of the woods yet.

A few months later, I had my hand operated on as an outpatient. Again, Kelly dropped me off at the doctor's office and picked me up when it was finished. I had to start physical therapy on that as well.

And during this time I had to get the occasional x-ray or MRI to see how my progress was going. I also got to know my physical therapist quite well. He was a nice guy, and he worked on my elbow and knee for a while. In fact, I got to know the whole staff, and they became my surrogate family while I was healing from everything. As soon as I could, I started walking without the cane. One time I took a fall in the middle of Santa Monica Blvd. during a busy day, which made me panic because I didn't want to injure myself again. I was a little terrified by falling given how much damage I'd sustained from a simple tumble. I was shaken and embarrassed, but I survived.

Though I still wanted to think the glass was half full, it was starting to look empty.

CHAPTER 12
THAT SILVER LINING THING

Whenever I'm at Disneyland, I both love and hate riding the Matterhorn. I love it because it's in the water, and I like twisting around. It's about as much as I can take in terms of rides, as I'm a real wuss when it comes to sitting in things that spin, flip, or jerk around. It's also scary because I'm so tall; I feel like my head is going to be knocked off when we are racing into the cave and that there will be a headless Deborah at the end of the ride. Of course, that never happens, but it sure feels like it will until the end, when I realize that I'm OK. After the ride is over, I need to find a bench to stretch out for a few moments, but I'm

OK. That is what this year of work was like. It was a great roller coaster going downhill, with the wind in my face. It felt great and freeing. But then the unexpected happened—something way out of left field that wasn't under my control, like a sudden, unexpected drop or turn on a coaster—and I got whipped around incredibly hard. And while I was at a standstill, on the ground waiting for help, my brain and body were in work mode, not in injured mode. I was jerked around into another whole world of emotions and stresses I wasn't ready for. I felt I had been thrown out of the car.

I lost my head.

That's sort of how I felt when I was on the ground waiting for the ambulance right after my accident. And during my recuperation, I still felt the need to keep working and not recovering. I didn't see people every day, I wasn't solving important problems, and I didn't have to handle any phone calls from overseas or make any deals for camera gear. I was finally still. The wheels were still spinning in my head, but my body wasn't moving, and I wasn't working. And since I tied my identity to how successful I was professionally, my self-esteem bottomed out.

There was a whole lot of white noise in my head.

I was desperate to get back to work and frightened of losing my contacts. I tried to rev myself back up again by keeping a schedule. Getting up, reading, doing my exercises, going on eBay to sell items, sending out résumés (even though the doctors had told me I wasn't supposed to be working), making calls, and coming up with show ideas. I was doing everything I could to stay in the game. But there were two very different voices in my head. One said things like, "You're going to be OK. You're the best. Don't worry." The other was filled with nagging doubt, and it kept asking me, "Who's going to hire you now? You fell on the job; you're toxic." I did what I could to suppress the negative feelings, but I felt like I was just trying to kid myself.

I didn't get out much during my recuperation. It was a pretty lonely time. I didn't want to let on that I was feeling the stress of what had happened, and so I stayed away from visitors and people calling. It was hard because anytime I finally wanted to go out, it would cost me money. Aside from Kelly, Rhonda, and Laura, I didn't have much of a support group. Kelly would come over and take me out to dinner or fix something at my house when I needed help. It felt like a lot of work to maintain the rest of my relationships and friendships. I had convinced myself that if I never called people, they would never call me. I got to the point where I felt that calling people was an intrusion, and I started to stay even further away.

I was quickly losing my positive-attitude battle, particularly when I heard that one of my old bosses had said, "Why would I hire her if she got injured on a show?" I started to feel like my career was pretty much over just when it seemed that I was really on a good career track. And I was older than most of my peers, primarily because it had taken me so long to finally decide what I wanted to pursue. When I started to think about my future and what I needed to do to secure it, my world fell apart. I was depressed, and I started gaining weight (something that was very easy for me to do) because I was eating a lot without working out. I would try to work out with my trainer, but it was just too hard. Too many different body parts hurt too much. Some days I could do sit-ups, and some days I couldn't. I really struggled with leg weights because of my knee. I finally gave up on working out altogether until I considered myself fixed and whole.

I was a drama queen having a pity party with myself.

But there was another voice in my head that kept asking a lot of questions. Was it worth it? Was I really happy? Was I getting where I wanted to be? Was I truly living my life? Did I even know who I was? Asking these questions slowed me down and gave me time to reflect. I began to embrace the downtime and actually started to answer some of those questions.

I also started to have some serious financial issues. The disability pay I was receiving while recuperating barely paid for my apartment, and I needed to be responsible. I tried to come up with a budget but was always coming up very short. I needed to do something. I had some savings, but those would be wiped out in no time. I started working with a former producer in a multilevel marketing company, but that started costing me more in terms of time than it rewarded me financially. A little after my elbow surgery, I received a letter from workers' compensation that said something about retaining a lawyer, which I decided to do. I was also having problems with my left shoulder. It was always tight, and I would have horrible headaches in my right eye; it felt like a pin was being stuck in my eyeball. And my whole upper back was as hard as a rock; I couldn't get comfortable. I started the inquiries to get that checked out with workers' comp, and my attorney followed up for me.

The 401k I had from a previous job had taken a hard hit in the stock market. It was $7,000 at one point, but by the time I arranged to cash it in, it was $900. But I needed the money. I also needed to move. So I had a large yard sale of stuff that was enough to get me moved into a one-bedroom apartment that would save me $600 a month.

Once my elbow had healed enough and I had some physical therapy, I was scheduled for wrist surgery. I must've landed on it when I fell because I had tissue damage and some torn ligaments. So I was in another cast, and I needed yet more physical therapy.

My new apartment was on an upper floor, which would've been OK if my knee didn't hurt all the time. But I learned to power through it. My knee was the one thing that seemed neglected, even though it had been the second most painful body part after I fell. There was no surgery scheduled for that, although I did get some physical therapy. I also started receiving permanent partial disability payments from workers' comp. I had started to take out money from my credit cards, figuring that I could pay them off as soon as I started working again. I have to thank *The Amazing Race* for my credit cards. I had used a lot of them on the show, and it helped my credit rating, giving me the ability to get more credit. It was also my downfall, but at this point, I didn't know what else to do. I still wasn't working.

Then I had an epiphany.

I got it. I was feeling sorry for myself, pouting around the house, and feeling miserable for myself. Yeah, I had a lot of problems, but I remembered hearing and reading that it is important to help other people rather than focusing on your own problems. Meaning I needed to stop focusing on "poor me" and do something for someone else—which is exactly what I did. A dear friend of mine became sick during my recovery. We had visited a couple of times, and I decided to pick her up one day and drive to Santa Barbara for lunch. We talked about our mutual woes, but we focused on what we were doing to make things better. It was a great afternoon. Knowing she was having financial difficulty, I decided to put together a party that was a fund raiser for her. I don't recall the details of how it all came about, but Laura helped spearhead the event and secured the location for the party, and a few other volunteers brought decorations and food. Together we raised about $2,500 for my friend. That felt great. Organizing the party made me realize just how lucky I was. My friend's illness was potentially life threatening. I just had some silly injuries. You gain a different perspective when you help those who need it. And I enjoyed doing this even more because she hadn't asked for it. It was a surprise.

I was beginning to put my drama-queen days behind me and see a glimmer of a silver lining. My head was still playing games with me, but I started to win the battle of positive thinking. I knew I would get over these injuries and be stronger for surviving them. I was going to laugh about it someday, just as I had promised myself while lying on the sidewalk a few months earlier.

But another injury that had nothing to do with my injuries from the shows caught up to me. Early on in my career, I'd experienced lower-back issues and had a deteriorating disk. At one point while working on *Wild Things*, I would sometimes have to crawl up the stairs to work (there was no elevator in the building). And on top of the shoulder pain and eye-piercing headaches, my back had started to act up again.

However, I was fortunate to have health insurance from a short-term job and was able to have a spinal fusion, complete with a couple of rods and screws as well as some cadaver bone to seal the disk from moving, sort of cementing it in place. I was beginning to feel better and waking up with a more positive attitude.

My friends came to see me and to bring me things while I was recuperating. I saw some of my poker buddies, friends from shows, and Rhonda and Kelly, and it felt good. The only problem was that I wasn't sure how I was going to get home. One of my poker buddies, Mark, volunteered to take me to my apartment, but I would need to climb up a lot of stairs to get to my unit. Once I was able to get up and go to the bathroom at the hospital, the nurses started trying to get me to walk up and down stairs. As soon as I could handle at least one stair, I was out the door.

Walking was very painful after the lower-back surgery, especially since I was also heavy, and I've always carried my weight in my stomach. But I was looking forward to finally getting back into fighting shape. And my mom was going to come out and help me for a week, since I would be mostly bedridden. The doctor suggested that someone should stay with me for at least a week in case I fell or something happened to me. This would mean that my mom would be with me over Thanksgiving.

My mom was helpful—except when I fell in the bathroom. My mom couldn't help me, but I managed to pull myself upright, although it took quite a lot of effort and screaming. Toward the end of my mom's stay, I was finally able to walk around a bit more and hang out in the living room. It was not much fun for her, but I appreciated her visit. It would be another month of recuperation before I could start working again, which meant that I probably wouldn't be working until after Christmas, in January or even February. So I decided to just hang in there financially until the New Year.

But then I received a letter just before Christmas.

Workers' comp had approved surgery for my shoulder. That was the good news. The bad news was that it could take me up to seven months to recuperate after that surgery. I was stunned. A chill shot up my spine. *Seven months?* I was in crazy debt, and I couldn't take out any more money. And at this point, my mom was helping me out. I couldn't take seven months of not working, living on state disability and the small checks I was receiving from workers' comp. I needed the surgery, but I couldn't afford to rent an apartment. I decided to move back home with my mom and have my surgery done in Indiana; I would spend the seven months of recuperation among old friends and family. So once again I had a big yard sale to get rid of as much stuff as possible (this was the third time in as many years). Then I packed up whatever was left for my move back home.

Rhonda and I took a road trip and drove back to Indiana at the end of January. It took about three days and two traffic citations in Arizona to get home. When we were pulled over by the highway patrol in Arizona, the officer asked me where I was going. I told him Indiana. He asked me what took me there, and I told him the I-40 to the I-69 into Indianapolis. Rhonda explained that he wanted to know *why* I was going to Indiana. I think he rewarded me with an extra ticket for that response. When we finally arrived home, I breathed a sigh of relief that I was no longer paying rent. I was now officially a "boomerang baby," another statistic. But I was feeling good about being home. I figured I would recuperate, get my head on straight, and return triumphantly to Hollywood, ready to take it on again.

I still had to recover from my back surgery before I could have the shoulder surgery. The doctor had told me to try physical therapy for my shoulder first to see if that fixed anything. It didn't. So in April I had my shoulder surgery. I don't know many of the details, but they did something like cutting part of my collar bone off so that it would fit against another bone in my shoulder. I have pictures of the little blade cutting through me. Pretty amazing. I was in and out of surgery in about four hours and then back home to recuperate.

I was also able to go back to work in a month, six months earlier than the recovery time outlined in the letter. Well, it had just been an estimate, I guess. I still had pain in my shoulder, probably from the surgery, but the headaches were gone. Someone had finally taken the pins out of my left eyeball.

I needed to go back to work to cover the mounting debt I had accumulated since being injured. I did get a job over the phone shortly after I began my job search, and I returned to Los Angeles.

But it didn't work out. Not just the job—which was terrible—but financially. It was hard to rent a place and a car while working in LA. I wasn't making any headway in paying my bills, and the only way to really get my debt down was to declare bankruptcy, which I refused to do. I don't believe in bankruptcy and was ready to fight it all the way.

And then I got another notice from workers' comp.

Workers' comp agreed that I could be retrained in another skill. I had requested this four years earlier, and in fact, I'd sent a proposal to my attorney outlining what I wanted to do and how much it would cost. I had wanted to be retrained as an Avid editor so that I could edit television shows. Editing was my first love while in film school, and my first job was as an assistant editor at Norton Air Force Base through a company one of my professors had started. But that dream was over for me. I felt like I was too old to start at the bottom and decided that real-estate appraising might be the way to go. Actually, Kelly had told me once that I would be great at it because of my attention to detail and love of numbers. So, on her recommendation, I decided to take the chance and learn something else. The kicker was that I couldn't work and study at the same time, so I ended my awful job and spent the next six months learning real-estate appraising. But after I had finished all of my classes and passed the state's test to become an official real-estate trainee, I was beyond broke and could not find a job in either real estate or production. I had two months of money left, period. If I could not find a job, then I would have to move back home.

I moved back home for the last time. But not before I had yet another yard sale where I tried to sell everything I owned. Since I don't like borrowing from friends or family, I had a raffle to raise money to pay my final rent and move back home.

I raised just enough money to pay rent, and my mom flew out to meet me. We drove my car back to Indiana. It was a lot of fun, and it reminded me of the many times our family had driven across country when moving from state to state.

If I were a baseball team, these would be my stats:

Number of marriages: 0
Number of marriage proposals: 2
Number of children: none that I know of (I hate it when a guy says that, so I just thought I'd try it on for size.)
Number of apartments since moving out of home: 10+
Number of cars owned: 7
Number of homes owned: 0
Number of roommates: 20+ (that's another book)
Number of surgeries: 8 and counting

And if I really wanted to feel bad about myself, all I had to do was think about all of my successful friends who had great homes and were much more financially stable than I was. You can really get depressed when you compare yourself to others. It's a bad idea.

But I had made the decision to smile. I don't know how to explain that, but while I wasn't feeling great about where I was in my life and had no idea what would happen to me (I truly felt that being homeless was a close option), I also knew in my heart that no matter what happened, it would be OK.

And if I had to do it over again, I totally would. I worked with some wonderful people and some not-so-wonderful people, and I learned from both. I encountered people and cultures I never would have come across if I hadn't made some daring choices early in my career. And while I did not choose to fall in December of 2001, what I've been able to do since then has been very rewarding. I was able to move back in with my mother during a stressful time in her life, after she lost her dog, and help take care of her while she was dealing with physical pain and disease. I was there when she went through a series of strokes and passed away. If it had not been for the fact that I was injured so badly that I needed to come home, I might never have had the chance to help my mom out as much as she had always helped me. So at least there was that silver lining.

Five years after my injury, I finally had to declare bankruptcy. I received a final settlement from workers' comp. I did get a job that was long term, so I did get "back on the horse," as they say.

I'm not sure where I will land, but I know that I will win. I may not be the richest or most successful person, but my family and friends are more important to me than any job. *I* am more important than any job. My perspective of work as the center of my life has changed. I now enjoy more than my work. I enjoy living life and being with people and fostering relationships. I even dabbled in improvisational comedy, something I hadn't done in years. Nothing to lose. Go for it. Just do it. Follow your fear. All these little sayings now go through my head.

I don't know if this revelation was because of my accident, getting older, or both, but I am grateful for the lesson, and I look forward to…well, everything. I think God gave me all that happened for a reason, and I am a much better person for going through it.

If I Google my great-grandfather, I can see his paintings, where they were auctioned, and how much they're worth. I can get a good idea of his contribution to his art. If I Google my grandfather, I can see the films his production company made for other companies; when he retired, he painted. I see the artwork of both my great-grandfather and my grandfather on my walls every day. If I Google my father, I can find kind things people have said about him and about the model airplanes he designed, even twenty years after his death.

I can only hope that when I'm Googled, there is something of value to be seen.

It has been my observation that we all go through at least one catastrophic event in our lives that changes us. I have seen it with many of the people I know, and it's how we handle those situations that show us who we are or who we can be. If I've learned anything, it is to take the time to heal, look around, and see who out there wants to help you and which people need your help. Try to protect yourself financially, if at all possible. The unexpected can happen, and it will.

It still happens to me.

And if you can, get disability insurance. It would've made a great difference in my life if I'd had it. I think Aflac would've been a good thing to have.

And always, always, always try to laugh about it later. I know I am finally doing that now.